Verse by Verse Commentary on the Books of

# 1-2-3 JOHN
# and JUDE

Enduring Word Commentary Series

By David Guzik

*The grass withers, the flower fades,*
*but the word of our God stands forever.*

Isaiah 40:8

*Commentary on 1-2-3 John and Jude*

**Copyright ©2005 by David Guzik**

Printed in the United States of America
or in the United Kingdom

ISBN 1-56599-031-5


**Enduring Word Media**

**USA**
Attention: Sheri Guzik
514 Jurupa Avenue
Redlands, CA 93065
USA

(909) 307-0688

**Europe**
Calvary Chapel Bibelschule
Eiserfelder Strasse 275
57080 Siegen
GERMANY

+49 (0)271 23 87 99 88


Electronic Mail: ewm@enduringword.com

Internet Home Page: www.enduringword.com

Scripture references, unless noted, are from the New King James Version of the Bible, copyright © 1979, 1980, 1982, Thomas Nelson, Inc., Publisher.

# Table of Contents

*Dedicated
with gratitude to
Nils-Erik and
Gunnel Ingrid
Bergström*

# 1 John 1 - Fellowship with God

*Most people understand that the important things in life are not things at all - they are the relationships we have. God has put a desire for relationship in every one of us, a desire He intended to be met with relationships with other people, but most of all, to be met by a relationship with Him. In this remarkable letter, John tells us the truth about relationships - and shows us how to have relationships that are real, for both now and eternity.*

A. The purpose of the letter: to bring you into relationship with God.

1. (1-2) John begins with the center of relationship: Jesus Christ.

**That which was from the beginning, which we have heard, which we have seen with our eyes, which we have looked upon, and our hands have handled, concerning the Word of life; the life was manifested, and we have seen, and bear witness, and declare to you that eternal life which was with the Father and was manifested to us.**

a. **That which was from the beginning**: The **beginning** John wrote of is not the beginning of this world; nor is it the beginning of creation. It is the beginning of Genesis 1:1 and John 1:1, the beginning there was before there was anything, when all there existed was God.

i. The beginning of Genesis 1:1 is simple: *In the beginning, God created the heavens and the earth.* The beginning of John 1:1 is profound: *In the beginning was the Word, and the Word was with God, and the Word was God.* John takes us back to this time in eternity past, to meet this One **which was from the beginning**.

ii. Whoever, or whatever, John wrote of, he said his subject was *eternal* and therefore was God because the subject existed before all else and was the source and basis of the existence of all things.

b. **Which we have heard, which we have seen with our eyes, which we have looked upon, and our hands have handled**: This indicates that this eternal being – the One **from the beginning** - came to earth, and John (among others) personally experienced this eternal One.

i. "We deliver nothing by hearsay, nothing by tradition, nothing from conjecture; we have had the fullest certainty of all that we write and preach." (Clarke) The idea is that this eternal subject of John has been audibly **heard**, physically **seen**, intently studied (**have looked upon**), and tangibly touched (**hands have handled**). This idea would have enormous implications for his readers.

ii. The implications were enormous because they said that this eternal God became accessible to man in the most basic way, a way that anyone could relate to. This eternal One can be known, and He has revealed Himself to us.

iii. The implications were enormous because they proved that John's words have the weight of eyewitness evidence. He did not speak of a myth or of a matter of clever story-telling. He carefully studied this eternal One and he knew whom he spoke about.

iv. Enormous because it debunked dangerous teachings that were creeping into the church, known as *Gnosticism*. Part of the teaching of Gnosticism was that though Jesus was God, He was not actually a physical man, but instead some kind of pseudo-physical phantom. Yet John declared, "I heard Him! I saw Him! I studied Him! I touched Him!"

c. **The Word of Life**: John identified this eternally existent being, who was physically present with John and others (note the repetition of **our**, and not "my"), as **the Word of Life**. This is the same *Logos* spoken of in John 1:1.

i. The idea of the *Logos* - of the **Word** - was important for John and for the Greek and Jewish worlds of his day. For the Jew, God was often referred to as *the Word* because they knew God perfectly revealed Himself in His Word. For the Greek, their philosophers had spoken for centuries about the *Logos* - the basis for organization and intelligence in the universe, the Ultimate Reason which controls all things.

ii. It is as if John said to everyone, "This *Logos* you have been talking about and writing about for centuries - well, we have heard Him, seen Him, studied Him, and touched Him. Let me now tell you about Him."

d. **The life was manifested**: This life was **manifested**, meaning that it was made actually and physically real. John solemnly testified as an eyewitness (**we have seen, and bear witness, and declare to you**) that this was the case. This was no fairy tale, no "Once upon a time" story. This was real, and John tells us about it as an eyewitness.

e. **Eternal life which was with the Father**: In calling Jesus **eternal life**, John remembered the words of Jesus (John 5:26, 6:48, and 11:25). He also repeated the idea expressed in his first words of this letter: that Jesus Himself is eternal, and therefore God.

> i. We can say that people are eternal, but we say this with the understanding that we mean they are eternal in the *future* sense - they will never perish, being immortal (John 5:29). Yet people are *not* eternal in the *past* sense; to say that something is eternal in the past sense is the same as saying it is equal to God or God's Word.

> ii. The eternal existence of Jesus is also declared in Micah 5:2 - *But you, Bethlehem Ephrathah, though you are little among the thousands of Judah, yet out of you shall come forth to Me the One to be Ruler in Israel, Whose goings forth are from of old, from everlasting.* The word *everlasting* here literally means, "beyond the vanishing point."

f. **Which was with the Father**: This refers to the *eternal* relationship between the Father and the Son. There was an eternal relationship of love and fellowship between the Father and the Son. Jesus referred to this in John 17:24: *"For You loved Me before the foundation of the world."*

> i. This eternal relationship is clearly described in the Scriptures, but we could also understand it from simple logic. If God is love (1 John 4:8) and God is eternal (Micah 5:2), we understand that love in isolation is meaningless. Love needs an object, and since there was a time before anything was created, there was a time when the only love in the universe was between the members of the Godhead: the Father, Son, and Holy Spirit.

g. **Was with the Father**: The word **with** indicates that this being, who is eternal, and is eternal life Himself, is distinct from the Father. John builds the New Testament understanding of the Trinity - that one God exists as three Persons, equal and one, yet distinct in their person.

> i. The Bible links together the names of the Father, Son, and Holy Spirit in a way that is unimaginable for other persons. We read, *Go therefore and make disciples of all the nations, baptizing them in the name of the Father and of the Son and of the Holy Spirit* (Matthew 28:19). Yet we would never say, "Go therefore and make disciples of all the nations, baptizing them in the name of the Father and of the Son and of Michael the Archangel."

> ii. We read, *The grace of the Lord Jesus Christ, and the love of God, and the communion of the Holy Spirit be with you all* (2 Corinthians 13:14). Yet we would never say, "The grace of the Lord Jesus Christ, and the love of the Apostle Paul, and the communion of the Holy Spirit be with you all."

iii. We read, *Elect according to the foreknowledge of God the Father, in sanctification of the Spirit, for obedience and sprinkling of the blood of Jesus Christ* (1 Peter 1:2). Yet we would never say, "*Elect according to the foreknowledge of God the Father, in sanctification of the Spirit, for obedience and sprinkling of the blood of the Apostle Peter.*"

2. (3) An invitation to relationship.

**That which we have seen and heard we declare to you, that you also may have fellowship with us; and truly our fellowship *is* with the Father and with His Son Jesus Christ.**

a. **That you may have fellowship with us; and truly our fellowship is with the Father and with His Son Jesus Christ**: The purpose of John's declaration about this eternally existent, physically present, *Word of life* who is God, yet is a person distinct from the Father, is to bring his readers into fellowship with both God's people and God Himself.

i. You can enjoy this fellowship even though you do not understand all the intricacies of the trinity. You can use your eyes even though you don't know every detail of how your vision works. You can know God and believe in Him as He has revealed Himself, even though you can't understand everything about His person or nature.

b. **Fellowship**: The idea of **fellowship** is one of the most important ideas in this letter of John's. It is the ancient Greek word *koinonia*, which speaks of a sharing, a communion, a common bond and common life. It speaks of a living, breathing, sharing, loving *relationship* with another person.

i. "This is one of the greatest statements of the New Testament, and it may safely be said that its greatness is created by the richness of the word which is the emphatic word, viz., *fellowship.*" (Morgan)

ii. "The Greek word *koinonia* is derived from the word *koinos*, which very literally means common, in the sense of being shared by all." (Morgan) The use of the word in Acts 2:44 is very helpful: *Now all who believed were together, and had all things in common.* The word *common* is the ancient Greek word *koinonia.*

iii. "Those who have a fellowship one with another, are those who share the same resources, and are bound by the same responsibilities. The idea becomes almost overwhelming when it is thus applied to the relationship which believing souls bear to the Father, and to His Son Jesus Christ. . . . The Father, His Son Jesus Christ, and all believers have all things in common. All the resources of each in the wondrous relationship are at the disposal of the others. Such is the grace of our God, and of His Son." (Morgan)

**c. Fellowship . . . with the Father and with His Son Jesus Christ**: This simple and bold statement means that one can have a relationship with *God*. This idea would surprise many of John's readers, and it should be astounding to us. The Greek mind-set highly prized the idea of *fellowship*, but restricted to men among men - the idea of such an intimate relationship with God was revolutionary.

> i. Jesus started the same kind of revolution among the Jews when He invited men to address God as *Father* (Matthew 6:9). We really can have a living, breathing relationship with God the Father, and with Jesus Christ. He can be not only our Savior, but also our friend and our closest relationship.

> ii. Actually, for many people this is totally unappealing. Sometimes it is because they don't know who God is, and an invitation to a "personal relationship with God" is about as attractive to them as telling an eighth-grader they can have a "personal relationship with the assistant principal." But when we know the greatness, the goodness, and the glory of God, we *want* to have a relationship with Him.

> iii. Other people turn from this relationship with God because they feel so distant from Him. They *want* a relationship with God, but feel so disqualified, so distant. They need to know what God has done to make this kind of relationship possible.

**d. Fellowship . . . with the Father and with His Son Jesus Christ**: The kind of relationship John described is only possible because Jesus is who John says He is in 1 John 1:1-2. If someone invited you to have a "personal relationship" with Napoleon, or Alexander the Great, or Abraham Lincoln - or even Moses or the Apostle Paul - you would think them foolish. One cannot even have a genuine "spiritual" relationship with a dead man. But with the eternal God who became man, we can have a relationship.

> i. The word **fellowship** has in it not only the idea of relationship, but of sharing a common life. When we have **fellowship** with Jesus, we will become more like Him.

> ii. The disciples did not have the close fellowship with Jesus when He walked this earth with them. As Jesus said to Philip at the very end of His earthly ministry, *"Have I been with you so long, and yet you have not known Me, Philip?"* (John 14:9) Their true fellowship was not created by material closeness to the material Jesus, *but by a work of the Holy Spirit after the finished work of Jesus on the cross.* Therefore we can enter into the *same* fellowship with God that the Apostles could enter.

e. **Our fellowship is with the Father and with His Son Jesus Christ**: We have the potential of a relationship of a *shared life* with **the Father and with His Son Jesus Christ**. It is as if the Father and the Son agree together to let us into their relationship of love and fellowship.

> i. This idea of a *shared life* is essential. This doesn't mean that when Jesus comes into our life He helps us to do the same things, but simply to do them better than before. We don't *add* Jesus to our life. We enter into a relationship of a *shared life* with Jesus. We share our life with Him, and He shares His life with us.

f. **That you also may have fellowship with us**: We may think it curious that John *first* considers fellowship with God's people; but this is often how people come to experience a relationship with God: they first encounter God through relationships with God's people.

> i. "When fellowship is the sweetest, your desire is the strongest that others may have fellowship with you; and when, truly, your fellowship is with the Father, and with his Son Jesus Christ, you earnestly wish that the whole Christian brotherhood may share the blessing with you." (Spurgeon)

g. **With the Father and with His Son Jesus Christ**: Here John finally names this being - eternally existent, physically present, the *Word of Life*, truly God (yet distinct from the Father) - it is God the **Son**, whose name is **Jesus**, who is the **Christ** (Messiah).

3. (4) The result of relationship.

**And these things we write to you that your joy may be full.**

a. **That your joy may be full**: The result of fellowship is fullness of **joy**. This **joy** is an abiding sense of optimism and cheerfulness based on *God*, as opposed to *happiness*, which is a sense of optimism and cheerfulness based on *circumstances*.

> i. John clearly echoed an idea Jesus brought before His disciples the night before His crucifixion. He wanted fullness of joy for them - even knowing that the cross was directly in front of them.
>
> - *These things I have spoken to you, that My joy may remain in you, and that your joy may be full* (John 15:11).
>
> - *Until now you have asked nothing in My name. Ask, and you will receive, that your joy may be full* (John 16:24).
>
> - *But now I come to You, and these things I speak in the world, that they may have My joy fulfilled in themselves* (John 17:13).

b. **That your joy may be full**: Fullness of joy is certainly *possible* for the Christian, but it is by no means *certain*. John wrote with the desire that believers would have fullness of joy - and if it were inevitable or very easy to have, he would not have written this.

> i. The Christian's joy is important, and assaulted on many fronts. External circumstances, moods and emotions, or sin can all take away our joy. Yet the Christian's joy is not found in the things of this world, as good as they might be. When John wrote about **these things**, he wrote about this relationship of fellowship and love we can share in with God the Father and the Son Jesus Christ.

> ii. Too many Christians are passive in their loss of joy. They need to realized it is a great loss and do everything they can to draw close to God and reclaim that fullness of joy. "If any of you have lost the joy of the Lord. I pray you do not think it a small loss." (Spurgeon)

4. Observations on this first portion of the book, which is one long sentence in the original manuscript.

a. John began with the *beginning* - the eternal God, who was before all things.

b. He told us that this God was physically manifested, and that he and others could testify to this as eyewitnesses.

c. He told us that this God is the *Word of life*, the *Logos*.

d. He told us that this God is distinct from the person of God the Father.

e. He told us that we may have fellowship with this God, and that we are often introduced into this fellowship with God by the fellowship of God's people.

f. He told us that this eternally existent God, the *Word of Life*, who was physically present with the the disciples and others (and present for fellowship), is God the Son, named Jesus Christ.

g. He told us that fellowship with Jesus leads to a life lived in fullness of joy.

h. We could say that in these four verses, John gave us enough to live our whole Christian life on. No wonder one commentator wrote, "Observe the note of wonder in the Apostle's language. Speech fails him. He labours for expression, adding definition to definition." (Expositor's)

B. John's message from God: dealing with sin and maintaining relationship.

1. (5) Sin and the nature of God.

**This is the message which we have heard from Him and declare to you, that God is light and in Him is no darkness at all.**

a. **This is the message**: This is a claim to authority. John isn't making this up; these are not his own personal opinions or ideas about God. This is God's message about Himself (**which we have heard from Him**), which John now reveals to us (**and declare to you**).

i. What John will tell us about God is what God has told us about Himself. We can't be confident in our own opinions or ideas about God unless they are genuinely founded on what God has said about Himself.

b. **God is light and in Him is no darkness at all**: We must begin our understanding of God here. John declares this on the simple understanding that God Himself is **light**; and light by definition has no **darkness at all** in it; for there to be darkness, there must be an *absence* of light.

i. A good definition of God is, "God is the only infinite, eternal, and unchangeable spirit, the perfect being in whom all things begin, and continue, and end." Another way of saying that God is *perfect* is to say that **God is light**.

ii. "LIGHT is the purest, the most subtle, the most useful, and the most diffusive of all God's creatures; it is, therefore, a very proper emblem of the *purity*, *perfection*, and *goodness* of the Divine nature." (Clarke)

iii. "There are spots in the sun, great tracts of blackness on its radiant disc; but in God is unmingled, perfect purity." (Maclaren)

c. **God is light and in Him is no darkness at all**: Therefore, if there is a problem with our fellowship with God, it is *our* fault. It is not the fault of God because there is no sin or **darkness** in Him **at all**.

i. Any approach to relationship with God that assumes, or even implies, that God might be wrong, and perhaps must be forgiven by us, is at its root blasphemous and directly contradicts what John clearly states here.

2. (6) God's sinlessness and our relationship with Him.

**If we say that we have fellowship with Him, and walk in darkness, we lie and do not practice the truth.**

a. **If we say that we have fellowship with Him**: John first deals with a *false claim* to fellowship. Based upon this, we understand that it is possible for some to *claim* a relationship with God that they do not have. We can also say that it is possible for someone to *think* they have a relationship with God that they do not have.

i. Many Christians are not aware of their true condition. They know they are saved, and have experienced conversion and have repented at some time in their life. Yet they do not live in true fellowship with God.

b. **And walk in darkness**: John speaks of a **walk** in darkness, indicating a *pattern* of living. This does not speak of an occasional lapse, but of a lifestyle of darkness.

c. **We lie and do not practice the truth**: God has *no darkness at all* (1 John 1:5). Therefore, if one claims to be in **fellowship** with God (a relationship of common relation, interest, and sharing), yet does **walk in darkness**, it is not a truthful claim.

i. The issue here is **fellowship**, not *salvation*. The Christian who temporarily walks in darkness is still saved, but not in **fellowship** with God.

ii. If John said "That is a lie," it means he thinks in terms of things being *true* or being *lies*. John sees things much more clearly than our sophisticated age does, which doesn't want to see anything in black or white, but everything in a pale shade of gray.

iii. In 2004, the governor of the state of New Jersey was caught in a scandal. Though he was a married man with children, he was also having a sexual relationship with a man. At the press conference he held to admit this, he began by saying: "My truth is that I am a gay American." Those were very carefully chosen words: *My truth*. In the thinking of the world today, I have my truth and you have your truth. But Jesus said, "I am the truth" and the Bible clearly tells us of a truth that is greater than any individual's feeling about it.

3. (7) The blessing of walking in the light.

**But if we walk in the light as He is in the light, we have fellowship with one another, and the blood of Jesus Christ His Son cleanses us from all sin.**

a. **But if we walk in the light**: This means to walk in a generally obedient life, without harboring known sin or resisting the conviction of the Holy Spirit on a particular point.

i. John's message here means that a **walk in the light** is *possible*. We know that on this side of eternity, *sinless perfection* is not possible. Yet we can still **walk in the light**, so John does mean perfect obedience.

ii. The Christian life is described as walking, which implies *activity*. Christian life feeds upon contemplation, but it displays itself in action. "Walking" implies action, continuity, and progress. Since God is active and walking, if you have fellowship with Him, you will also be active and walking.

b. **As He is in the light**: Since God is light (1 John 1:5), when we walk in the light we walk where He is. We are naturally together with Him in fellowship.

c. **We have fellowship with one another**: We would have expected John to say, "We have fellowship with God." That is true, but already in the idea of walking together with God in the light. John wants to make it clear that fellow Christians who walk in the light enjoy fellowship with each other.

> i. This leads to an important idea: if we do *not* **have fellowship with one another**, then one party or both parties are not walking **in the light**. Two Christians who are in right relationship with God will also naturally be in right relationship with each other.

d. **The blood of Jesus Christ His Son cleanses us from all sin**: As we **walk in the light** we also enjoy the continual cleansing of Jesus. This is another indication that John does not mean sinless perfection by the phrase **walk in the light**; otherwise, there would be no sin to cleanse in this ongoing sense.

> i. We need a continual cleansing because the Bible says we continually sin and fall short of the glory of God (Romans 3:23). Even though Christians have been cleansed in an important general sense, our "feet" need cleaning (John 13:10).

> ii. The verb form John used in *cleanses* **us from all sin** is in the present tense, not in the future tense. We can do more than merely *hope* we will one day be cleansed. Because of what Jesus did on the cross for me, I can be cleansed *today*.

> iii. "Observe, yet again, that in the verse there is no hint given of any emotions, feelings, or attainments, as co-operating with the blood to take away sin. Christ took the sins of his people and was punished for those sins as if he had been himself a sinner, and so sin is taken away from us; but in no sense, degree, shape or form, is sin removed by attainments, emotions, feelings or experiences." (Spurgeon)

e. **The blood of Jesus Christ**: This continual cleansing is ours by the **blood of Jesus**. This does not mean the actual drops or molecules of His literal blood, but His literal death in our place and the literal wrath of the Father He endured on our behalf. The **blood of Jesus Christ** paid the penalty for all our sins - past, present, and future.

> i. The work of Jesus on the cross doesn't only deal with the *guilt* of sin that might send us to hell. It also deals with the *stain* of sin which hinders our continual relationship with God. We need to come to God often with the simple plea, "cleanse me with the blood of Jesus."

Not because we haven't been cleansed before, but because we need to be continually cleansed to enjoy continual relationship.

ii. "'The blood' is more specific than 'the death' would be, for 'the blood' denotes sacrifice. It is always the blood that is shed." (Lenski)

iii. "Observe, here is nothing said about rites and ceremonies. It does not begin by saying, 'and the waters of baptism, together with the blood of Jesus Christ, his Son, cleanseth us,' - not a word, whether it shall be the sprinkling in infancy, or immersion of believers, nothing is said about it-it is the blood, the blood only, without a drop of baptismal water. Nothing is here said about sacraments - what some call 'the blessed Eucharist' is not dragged in here - nothing about eating bread and drinking wine - it is the blood, nothing but the blood." (Spurgeon)

iv. "Does my walking in the light take away my sins? Not at all. I am as much a sinner in the light as in the darkness, if it were possible for me to be in the light without being washed in the blood. Well, but we have fellowship with God, and does not having fellowship with God take away sin? Beloved, do not misunderstand me - no man can have fellowship with God unless sin be taken away; but his fellowship with God, and his walking in light, does not take away his sin - not at all. The whole process of the removal of sin is here, 'And the blood of Jesus Christ his Son cleanseth us from all sin.' " (Spurgeon)

f. **From all sin**: We can be cleansed, by the blood of Jesus, from **all sin**. The sin we inherited from Adam, the sin we committed as kids, the sins of our growing up; sins against our father, against our mother, against our brother and sister; sins against our husbands or wives, against our children; sins against our employers or our employees, sins against our friends and our enemies; lying, stealing, cheating, adultery, swearing, drugs, booze, promiscuity, murder; sins that haunt us every day, sins we didn't even know we did - **all sin** can be cleansed by the blood of Jesus.

i. Sin is the hindrance to fellowship and the blood of Jesus, received by faith as the payment for our sin, solves the problem of sin and opens the way to fellowship with God.

- You can't come to fellowship with God through philosophical speculation. You can't come to fellowship with God through intellectual education.

- You can't come to fellowship with God through drugs or entertainment.

- You can't come to fellowship with God through scientific investigation.

- You can *only* come to fellowship with God by dealing with your sin problem through the blood of Jesus.

ii. We might say that the *only* sin that cannot be cleansed by the **blood of Jesus** is the sin of continuing to reject that blood as payment for sin.

4. (8-10) The presence of sin, the confession of sin, and the cleansing from sin.

**If we say that we have no sin, we deceive ourselves, and the truth is not in us. If we confess our sins, He is faithful and just to forgive us *our* sins and to cleanse us from all unrighteousness. If we say that we have not sinned, we make Him a liar, and His word is not in us.**

a. **If we say we have no sin**: John has introduced the ideas of walking in the light and being cleansed from sin. But he did not for a moment believe that a Christian can become sinlessly perfect.

i. To *think* this of ourselves is to **deceive ourselves**, and to *say* this of ourselves is to lie - **the truth is not in us**.

ii. "Our deceitful heart reveals an almost Satanic shrewdness in self-deception . . . If you say you have no sin you have achieved a fearful success, you have put out your own eyes, and perverted your own reason!" (Spurgeon)

iii. There are few people today who think they are sinlessly perfect, yet not many really think of themselves as *sinners*. Many will say "I make mistakes" or "I'm not perfect" or "I'm only human," but usually they say such things to *excuse* or *defend*. This is different from knowing and admitting "I am a sinner."

iv. To say that **we have no sin** puts us in a dangerous place because God's grace and mercy is extended to *sinners*, not to "those who make mistakes" or "I'm only human" or "no one is perfect" people, but *sinners*. We need to realize the victory and forgiveness that comes from saying, "I am a sinner - even a great sinner - but I have a Savior who cleanses me from all sin."

b. **If we confess our sins**: Though sin is present, it need not remain a hindrance to our relationship with God - we may find complete cleansing (**from *all* unrighteousness**) as we confess our sins.

i. To **confess** means, "to say the same as." When we confess our sin, we are willing to say (and believe) the same thing about our sin that God says about it. Jesus' story about the religious man and the sinner who prayed before God illustrated this; the Pharisee bragged about how righteous he was, while the sinner just said *God be merciful to me a* *sinner* (Luke 18:10-14). The one who confessed his sin was the one who agreed with God about how bad he was.

ii. **Confess** translates a verb in the present tense. The meaning is that we should *keep on confessing* our sin - instead of referring to a "once-for-all" confession of sin at our conversion.

iii. You don't have to go to a confessional to confess your sin. When you are baptized, you are confessing your sin by saying you needed to be cleansed and reborn. When you receive communion, you confess your sin by saying you need the work of Jesus on the cross to take your sin away. But of course, we need to confess our sin in the most straightforward way: by admitting to God that what we have done is *sin*, and by asking for His divine forgiveness, based on what Jesus has done on the cross for us.

iv. Our sins are not forgiven *because* we confess. If this were the case - if forgiveness for a sin could only come where there was confession - then we would all be damned because it would be impossible for us to confess every sin we ever commit. We are forgiven because our punishment was put upon Jesus, we are cleansed by His blood.

v. However, confession is still vital to maintain *relationship* with God, and this is the context John speaks from. As God convicts us of sin that is hindering our fellowship with Him, we must confess it and receive forgiveness and cleansing for our relationship with God to continue without hindrance.

vi. Confession must be *personal*. To say, "God, if we have made any mistakes, forgive us" isn't confession, because it isn't *convinced* (saying "*if* we made"), it isn't *personal* (saying "if *we* made"), it isn't *specific* (saying "if we made *any*"), and it isn't *honest* (saying "mistakes").

c. **He is faithful and just to forgive us**: Because of Jesus' work, the righteousness of God is our *friend* - insuring that we will be forgiven because Jesus paid the penalty of our sin. God is being **faithful and just** to forgive us in light of Jesus.

i. "The text means just this - Treat God truthfully, and he will treat you truthfully. Make no pretensions before God, but lay bare your soul, let him see it as it is, and then he will be faithful and just to forgive you your sins and to cleanse you from all unrighteousness." (Spurgeon)

ii. The promise of 1 John 1:9 shouldn't lead us *into* sin, saying "Hey, I'll go ahead and sin because God will forgive me." It should lead us *out of* sin, knowing that God could only be **faithful and just to forgive us our sins** because the wrath we deserved was poured out on the sin. Since each sin carries with it its own measure of wrath, so there is a sense in which each sin we commit added to the agony of Jesus on the cross.

iii. There is no *more sure* evidence that a person is out of fellowship with God than for someone to contemplate or commit sin with the idea, "I can just ask for forgiveness later." Since God is light and in Him is no darkness at all, we can be assured that the person who commits sin with this idea is not in fellowship with God.

d. **If we say that we have not sinned**: If we deny the presence of sin, we are self-deceived and are denying God's Word. Yet, though sin is always present, so is its remedy - so sin need never be a hindrance to our relationship with God.

i. The idea that **His word is not in us** is related to the idea that Jesus is *the Word of life* (1 John 1:1); if we refuse to see sin in us, we show that Jesus is not in us.

ii. "No man was ever kept out of God's kingdom for his confessed badness; many are for their supposed goodness." (Trapp)

# *1 John 2 - Hindrances to Fellowship with God*

A. Fellowship and the problem of sin.

1. (1a) A purpose of John in writing this letter: **that you may not sin.**

**My little children, these things I write to you, that you may not sin.**

a. **These things I write to you, that you may not sin**: 1 John 1:8 made it clear that sin is a fact (at least an occasional fact) in the life of the Christian. 1 John 1:9 makes it clear that there is always forgiveness for confessed sin. Yet, John wants it also to be clear that the Christian should be concerned about sin. One reason in writing this letter was **that you may not sin.**

i. John previously rebuked the idea that we can become sinlessly perfect (1 John 1:8). At the same time, he wants to make it clear that we do not *have* to sin. God does not *make* the believer sin.

b. **That you may not sin**: This is God's desire for the believer. If sin is inevitable for us, it is not because God has decreed that we *must* sin. All the resources for spiritual victory are ours in Jesus Christ and that resource is never withdrawn.

i. John addresses this because of the issue of *relationship* with God (1 John 1:3), and the fact that sin can break our fellowship with God (1 John 1:6). He wants to make it clear that God has not made a system where we *must* break fellowship with Him through sin.

ii. The weakness comes in our flesh, which is not consistently willing to rely on Jesus for victory over sin. God promises that one day the flesh will be perfected through resurrection.

2. (1b-2) Help for the sinner and the restoration of fellowship.

**And if anyone sins, we have an Advocate with the Father, Jesus Christ the righteous. And He Himself is the propitiation for our sins, and not for ours only but also for the whole world.**

a. **We have an Advocate**: God's desire is that *you may not sin*. Yet if we do, there is provision made - **an Advocate**, a defense lawyer on our side. Our **Advocate** is Jesus Christ Himself.

i. Lenski on the ancient word for **Advocate**: "Demosthenes uses it to designate the friends of the accused who voluntarily step in and personally urge the judge to decide in his favor."

b. **We have an Advocate**: Jesus is our defender, even when we sin *now*. God is not shocked by human behavior. He has seen it all in advance. He didn't forgive us at one time to later say, "Look what they did now! If I would have known they would go and do that, I would have never forgiven them." His forgiveness is available to us *now*.

i. It is as if we stand as the accused in the heavenly court, before our righteous Judge, God the Father. Our Advocate stands up to answer the charges: "He is completely guilty your honor. In fact, he has even done worse than what he is accused of, and now makes full and complete confession before You." The gavel slams, and the Judge asks, "What should his sentence be?" Our Advocate answers, "His sentence shall be death; he deserves the full wrath of this righteous court." All along, our accuser Satan, is having great fun at all this. We are guilty! We admit our guilt! We see our punishment! But then, our Advocate asks to approach the bench. As he draws close to the Judge, he simply says: "Dad, this one belongs to Me. I paid his price. I took the wrath and punishment from this court that he deserves." The gavel sounds again, and the Judge cries out, "Guilty as charged! Penalty satisfied!" Our accuser starts going crazy. "Aren't you even going to put him on probation?" "No!" the Judge shouts. "The penalty has been completely paid by My Son. There is nothing to put him on probation for." Then the Judge turns to our Advocate, and says, "Son, you said this one belongs to You. I release him into Your care. Case closed!"

c. **We have an Advocate with the Father, Jesus Christ the righteous**: We may think that our sin sets God *against* us. But God's love is so great that in His love, He went to the ultimate measure to make us able to stand in the face of His holy righteousness. Through Jesus, God can be *for us* even when we are guilty sinners.

i. A human defense lawyer argues for the innocence of his client. But our **Advocate**, Jesus Christ, admits our guilt - and then enters His plea on our behalf, as the one who has made an atoning sacrifice for our sinful guilt.

ii. **Jesus Christ the righteous** means that Jesus is fully qualified to serve as our Advocate, because He Himself is sinlessly perfect. He has passed heaven's bar exam, and is qualified to represent clients in heaven's court of law.

iii. We need Jesus as our **Advocate** because Satan accuses us before God (Revelation 12:10). We need to distinguish between the condemning accusation of Satan and the loving conviction of the Holy Spirit.

d. **And He Himself is the propitiation for our sins**: This means that Jesus is the one who atones for and takes away our sins, and not only our sins, but also the sins of the **whole world**.

i. **Propitiation** has the idea of presenting a gift to the gods, so as to turn away the displeasure of the gods. The Greeks thought of this in the sense of man essentially bribing the gods into doing favors for man. But in the Christian idea of propitiation, God **Himself** presents **Himself** (in Jesus Christ) as that which will turn away His righteous wrath against our sin.

ii. Alford on **propitiation**: "The word implies that Christ has, as our sin-offering, reconciled God and us by nothing else but by His voluntary death as a sacrifice: has by this averted God's wrath from us."

e. **And not for ours only but also for the whole world**: Though Jesus made His propitiation **for the whole world**, yet the whole world is not saved and in fellowship with God. This is because *atonement* does not equal *forgiveness*. The Old Testament Day of Atonement (Leviticus 16:34) demonstrates this, when the sin of all Israel was atoned for every year at the Day of Atonement, yet not all of Israel was saved.

i. The words "**but also for the whole world**" announce to the world that God has taken care of the sin problem by the propitiation of Jesus Christ. Sin *need not* be a barrier between God and man, if man will receive the propitiation God has provided in Jesus.

ii. "The reason of the insertion of the particular here, is well given by Luther: 'It is a patent fact that thou too are part of the whole world: so that thine heart cannot deceive itself and think, The Lord died for Peter and Paul, but not for me.' " (Alford)

3. (3-6) The fruit of fellowship.

**Now by this we know that we know Him, if we keep His commandments. He who says, "I know Him," and does not keep His commandments, is a liar, and the truth is not in him. But whoever keeps His word, truly the love of God is perfected in him. By this we know that we are in Him. He who says he abides in Him ought himself also to walk just as He walked.**

a. **Now by this we know that we know Him**: The evidence of someone knowing God, and fellowship with Him is that he does **keep His commandments**. A simple, loving obedience is a natural result of fellowship with God.

> i. We have a gracious Advocate in heaven. We have an open invitation to restoration through confession. Yet these things do not make the converted man careless about the commandments. God changes the heart at conversion and writes His law upon our heart.

> ii. "Those men who think that God's grace, when fully, fairly, and plainly preached, will lead men into sin, know not what they say, nor whereof they affirm . . . Shall I hate God because he is kind to me? Shall I curse him because he blesses me? I venture to affirm that very few men reason thus." (Spurgeon)

b. **A liar, and the truth is not in him**: The truth of this is so certain that if one does not live a life marked by obedience, his claim to fellowship (the experiential knowledge) with God can be fairly challenged.

> i. **I know Him**: "Do distinguish, however, between knowing about Christ and knowing Christ. We may know very much about many of our great men, though we do not know them. Now, it will never save a soul to know about Christ. The only saving knowledge is to know him, his very self, and to trust him, the living Savior, who is now at the right hand of God." (Spurgeon)

c. **But whoever keeps His word, truly the love of God is perfected in him**: John also makes the link between our obedience and our love for God. A **perfected** (the idea is *mature*) love for God will show itself in obedience, and the presence of this obedience and love gives us assurance that we are in Jesus (**By this we know we are in Him**).

> i. Mark it, when one becomes a Christian, there is a change in his relationship with sin. Sin is not eliminated in the believer until he comes to glory, but his relationship to sin is changed when he truly become a Christian.

> - A Christian no longer loves sin as he once did.
> - A Christian no longer brags about his sin as he once did.
> - A Christian no longer plans to sin as he once did.
> - A Christian no longer fondly remembers his sin as he once did.
> - A Christian never fully enjoys his sin as he once did.
> - A Christian no longer is comfortable in habitual sin as he once was.

ii. *"The Christian no longer loves sin;* it is the object of his sternest horror: he no longer regards it as a mere trifle, plays with it, or talks of it with unconcern . . . Sin is dejected in the Christian's heart, though it is not ejected. Sin may enter the heart, and fight for dominion, but it cannot sit upon the throne." (Spurgeon)

d. **He who says he abides in Him ought himself also to walk just as He walked**: The thought is brought around to a full circle. When we are abiding in Jesus, we will **walk just as He walked** - live lives of obedience and love. When we want to **walk just as He walked**, we need to begin by abiding in Him.

i. **To walk just as He walked**: We aren't called to imitate the way Jesus walked on water, but His every-day walk with God the Father. The spiritual power evident in the life of Jesus flowed from a faithful, regular, disciplined life of fellowship and obedience.

ii. "The point here is that the one who knows God will increasingly lead a righteous life, for God is righteous. It does not mean that he will be sinless; John has already shown that anyone who claims this is lying. It simply means that he will be moving in a direction marked out by the righteousness of God. If he does not do this, if he is not increasingly dissatisfied with and distressed by sin, he is not God's child." (Boice)

4. (7-11) The absolute imperative of love.

**Brethren, I write no new commandment to you, but an old commandment which you have had from the beginning. The old commandment is the word which you heard from the beginning. Again, a new commandment I write to you, which thing is true in Him and in you, because the darkness is passing away, and the true light is already shining. He who says he is in the light, and hates his brother, is in darkness until now. He who loves his brother abides in the light, and there is no cause for stumbling in him. But he who hates his brother is in darkness and walks in darkness, and does not know where he is going, because the darkness has blinded his eyes.**

a. **Brethren, I write no new commandment to you . . . a new commandment I write to you**: The commandment John wrote of was at the same time both **old** (in the sense that it was preached to the brethren their whole Christian lives) and **new** (in the sense that it was called the *new commandment* by Jesus in John 13:34).

i. The **new commandment** "to love" that Jesus spoke of in John 13:34 was really new for several reasons. One of the most important reasons was that Jesus *displayed* a kind of love never seen before, a love we were to imitate.

ii. The cross points in four directions to show that the love of Jesus is:

*Wide* enough to include every human being.
*Long* enough to last through all eternity.
*Deep* enough to reach the most guilty sinner.
*High* enough to take us to heaven.

This is a new love, a love the world had never really seen before the work of Jesus on the cross.

b. **Because the darkness is passing away, and the true light is already shining**: The new commandment of love is necessary because of the darkness that marked humanity, especially the Gentiles. This was before the **true light** illuminated the finished work of Jesus.

c. **He who says he is in the light, and hates his brother, is in darkness until now**: Previously in this chapter, John examined us according to the moral measure of our walk with God. Later he will examine us according to doctrine as a measure of our walk with God. Now he examines us *according to our love for other Christians* as a measure of our walk with God.

i. Just as our relationship to sin and our obedience is a measure of our fellowship with God, so also is our love for God's people. If we say that we are **in the light** yet hate our brother, then our claim to fellowship with the God who is light (1 John 1:5) is hollow. But the one who *does* love his brother shows that he **abides in the light** and is not stumbling.

ii. "It seems plain that the expression here is not the same as '*his neighbor*,' seeing that St. John is writing to Christians, and treating of their *fellowship with one another*." (Alford)

iii. Sometimes it is easy to think, "Following Jesus would be easy if it weren't for all the Christians." And many, many Christians live as the walking wounded, crippled by the scars other Christians have inflicted on them. Yet this measure still stands. If we can't love each other, then we have no way to claim a real love for God. Our relationship with God can be measured by our love for other Christians.

iv. On the one hand, God is merciful in requiring this, because we are measured by how we love other Christians, not those who are not Christians. On the other hand, God gives us a particularly difficult measure, because we often - perhaps rightly - expect much more from our Christian friends and associates.

d. **But he who hates his brother is in darkness and walks in darkness**: The point is plain. If we lose love then we lose everything. There is nothing left. You can do all the right things, believe all the right truths, but if you do not love other Christians, then all is lost. The three tests - moral, doctrinal, and love - all stand together, like the legs on a three-legged stool.

i. It is all too easy for people to place "ministry" or "being right" above love in the body of Christ. We *must* do ministry, and we *must* be right, but we *must* do it all in love - if not in perfect actions, then following with proper repentance.

e. **Does not know where he is going, because the darkness has blinded his eyes**: Knowing the importance that Jesus placed on our love for each other, John will go so far as to say that if we **hate** our brother, we are walking in darkness, and are unable to see - we have been blinded.

i. Remember that hatred can also be expressed by indifference; true love will demonstrate itself for one another.

ii. We can be sure that John himself lived this life of love, but he wasn't always this way. John himself learned love at this point, for early in his life he was known as one of the "sons of thunder." He once wanted to call down fire from heaven upon those who rejected Jesus (Luke 9:54).

B. John addresses his readers according to their measure of spiritual maturity.

1. (12) **Little children**, who have their sins forgiven.

**I write to you, little children, because your sins are forgiven you for His name's sake.**

a. **I write to you, little children**: We each begin the Christian life as **little children**. When we are in this state spiritually, it is enough for us to know and be amazed at the forgiveness of our sins and all it took for God to forgive us righteously in Jesus Christ.

b. **Because your sins are forgiven you for His name's sake**: This is something to rejoice in. If we do not rejoice in this, something is wrong. We probably fail to see the badness of our sin and the greatness of His forgiveness. When we see how great our sin is, and how great the cost was to gain us forgiveness, we are *obsessed* with gratitude at having been forgiven.

c. **Little children**: This forgiveness is the special joy of God's **little children**, because God's forgiveness does not come by degrees. Even the youngest Christian is completely forgiven. They will never be "more forgiven." Forgiveness is God's gift, not man's achievement.

i. Note it well: **forgiven you for *His name's sake***. The reasons for forgiveness are not found in us, but in God.

2. (13a) **Fathers**, who have an experiential knowledge of Jesus Christ.

**I write to you, fathers, because you have known Him *who is* from the beginning.**

a. **I write to you, fathers**: Just as surely as there are *little children*, there are also **fathers**. These are men and women of deep, long spiritual standing. They have the kind of walk with God that doesn't come overnight. These are like great oak trees in the Lord, that have grown big and strong through the years.

b. **You have known Him**: This is what spiritual maturity has its roots in. It is not so much in an intellectual knowledge (though that is a part of it), but more so in the depth of fellowship and relationship we have with Jesus. There is no substitute for years and years of an experiential relationship with Jesus.

3. (13b) **Young men**, who have known spiritual victory.

**I write to you, young men, because you have overcome the wicked one.**

a. **I write to you, young men**: As much as there are *little children* and *fathers*, so also there are **young men**. These are men and women who are no longer little children, but still not yet fathers. They are the "front-line" of God's work among His people.

i. "The proper attribute of youth is, to carry on the active parts of life - if soldiers, to be engaged in all active service." (Alford)

b. **Because you have overcome the wicked one**: They are engaged in battle with **the wicked one**. We don't send our little children out to war, and we don't send our old men to the front lines. The greatest effort, the greatest cost, and the greatest strength are expected of the **young men**.

i. For this reason, many have sought to stay in spiritual childhood as long as possible. This is wrong. It is like being a draft-dodger or a vagrant. We expect children to not fight in wars and to be supported by others, but we don't expect it of adults.

c. **Overcome the wicked one**: These **young men** have overcome the spiritual foes that would seek to destroy their spiritual life. They know what it is to battle against Satan and his emissaries as a partner with God.

4. (13c) **Little children**, who know the Father.

**I write to you, little children, because you have known the Father.**

a. **Because you have known the Father**: In this first stage of spiritual growth, we sink our roots deep in the Fatherly love and care of God. We know Him as our caring Father, and see ourselves as His dependent children.

i. "And do you not glory in him? Little children when they begin to talk, and go to school, how proud they are of their father! Their father is the greatest man that ever lived: there never was the like of him. You may talk to them of great statesmen, or great warriors, or great princes, but these are all nobodies: their father fills the whole horizon of their being. Well, so it certainly is with us and our Father God." (Spurgeon)

b. **Little children**: John uses different words for **little children** in verses 12 and 13 (*teknia* and *paidia*, respectively). *Teknia* has more of an emphasis on a child's relationship of dependence on a parent, while *paidia* has more of an emphasis on a child's immaturity and need for instruction.

5. (14a) **Fathers**, who have an experiential knowledge of Jesus Christ.

**I have written to you, fathers, because you have known Him *who is* from the beginning.**

a. **Because you have known Him who is from the beginning**: The repetition of the same idea from 14a shows that it should be emphasized. The relationship with Jesus Christ that people at this stage of spiritual growth have is both true and deep.

b. **I have written to you**: Sometimes we might think, "Well, isn't there more? It's fine for these **fathers** to know Jesus, but shouldn't they go beyond?" This repetition reminds us that there is no beyond.

i. Paul, in his letter to the Philippians, could say that he counted all his previous spiritual achievements as rubbish, compared to the surpassing greatness of just knowing Jesus. *That I may know Him* is the powerful way Paul phrased it in Philippians 3:10.

6. (14b) **Young men**, who are strong and know spiritual victory.

**I have written to you, young men, because you are strong, and the word of God abides in you, and you have overcome the wicked one.**

a. **I have written to you, young men**: Again, the repetition of the idea indicates emphasis. Not only have the **young men . . . overcome the wicked one**, but they have done it through the strength that comes to them through the **word of God**. God's Word is our source of spiritual strength.

i. Do you consider yourself one of the **young men** spiritually? Then are you **strong**? Are you putting your strength to some spiritual use? Do you resent that your strength is tested and developed by God?

b. **The word of God abides in you**: These **young men**, who had gained some measure of spiritual maturity, were known by the fact that God's Word *lived* in them. The Word of God had made itself at home in their hearts.

C. An attack on our relationship with God: worldliness.

1. (15) The problem of worldliness.

**Do not love the world or the things in the world. If anyone loves the world, the love of the Father is not in him.**

a. **Do not love the world**: John has told us that if we walk in sin's darkness and claim to be in fellowship with God, we are lying (1 John 1:6). Now John points out a specific area of sin that especially threatens our fellowship with God: worldliness, to **love the world**.

b. **Do not love the world or the things in the world**: The **world**, in the sense John means it here, is not the global earth. Nor is it the mass of humanity, which God Himself loves (John 3:16). Instead it is the community of sinful humanity that is united in rebellion against God.

i. One of the first examples of this idea of the **world** in the Bible helps us to understand this point. Genesis 11 speaks of human society's united rebellion against God at the tower of Babel. At the tower of Babel, there was an *anti-God leader* of humanity (whose name was Nimrod). There was *organized rebellion against God* (in disobeying the command to disperse over the whole earth). There was *direct distrust of God's word and promise* (in building what was probably a water-safe tower to protect against a future flood from heaven).

ii. The whole story of the tower of Babel also shows us another fundamental fact about the world system. The world's progress, technology, government, and organization can make man *better off*, but not *better*. Because we like being better off, it is easy to fall in love with the world.

iii. Finally, the story of the tower of Babel shows us that the world system - as impressive and winning as it appears to be - will *never* win out over God. The Lord defeated the rebellion at the tower of Babel easily. The world system will *never* win out over God.

c. **Do not love the world**: That is, we are not to love either the world's system or its way of doing things. There is a secular, anti-God or ignoring-God way of doing things that characterizes human society, and it is easy to **love the world** in this sense.

i. Notice what the world wants from us: **love**. This love is expressed in time, attention, and expense. We are encouraged and persuaded to give our time, attention, and money to the things of this world instead of the things of God.

ii. If you love the world, there are rewards to be gained. You may find a place of prestige, of status, of honor, of comfort. The world system knows how to reward its lovers.

iii. At the same time, even at their best the rewards that come from this world last only as long as we live. The problem is that though we gain prestige, status, honor, and comfort of this world, we lose the prestige, status, honor, and comfort of heaven.

d. **Or the things in the world**: This isn't so much a warning against a love for the beauty of the world God created (though we must always love the Creator instead of the creation). Instead, it is more of a warning against loving the material things which characterize the world system.

i. The world buys our love with the great **things** it has to give us. Cars, homes, gadgets, and the status that goes with all of them, can really make our hearts at home in the world.

e. **If anyone loves the world, the love of the Father is not in him**: Simply, love for the world is incompatible with love for the Father. Therefore if one claims to love God and yet loves the world, there is something wrong with his claim to love God.

i. Through the centuries, Christians have dealt with the magnetic pull of the world in different ways. At one time it was thought that if you were a really committed Christian and really wanted to love God instead of the world, you would leave human society and live as a monk or a nun out in a desolate monastery.

ii. This approach, and other approaches that seek to take us *out of* the world, have two problems. The first problem is that we bring the world with us into our monastery. The other problem is that Jesus intended us to be *in the world* but not *of the world*. We see this in His prayer for us in John 17:14-18.

2. (16) The character of the world.

**For all that *is* in the world; the lust of the flesh, the lust of the eyes, and the pride of life; is not of the Father but is of the world.**

a. **For all that is in the world**: The character of the world expresses itself through the **lust of the flesh**, the **lust of the eyes**, and the **pride of life**. These lusts seek to draw our own flesh away into sin and worldliness.

i. The idea behind **the pride of life** is someone who lives for superiority over others, mostly by impressing others through outward appearances - even if by deception.

ii. To get an idea of how the world works, think of the advertising commercials you most commonly remember. They probably make a powerful appeal to the **lust of the flesh**, the **lust of the eyes**, or to the **pride of life**. Many successful ads appeal to all three.

b. **The lust of the flesh, the lust of the eyes, and the pride of life**: In listing these aspects of the world, John may have in mind the first pursuit of worldliness, that of Eve in the Garden of Eden (Genesis 3:6).

i. Of Eve in the Garden of Eden, it is said that she took of the forbidden fruit when she *saw that the tree was good for food*. She thought about how good the fruit would taste, how it would satisfy her flesh. She went after the **lust of the flesh**.

ii. Of Eve in the Garden of Eden, it is said that she took of the forbidden fruit when she saw that the fruit *was pleasant to the eyes*. She saw how pretty and desirable it was, and it pleased her artistic sense. She went after the **lust of the eyes**.

iii. Of Eve in the Garden of Eden, it is said that she took of the forbidden fruit when she believed that it was *desirable to make one wise*. How smart the fruit would make her! How her husband would admire her! She went after the **pride of life**.

c. **Is not of the Father but is of the world**: This explains why the **lust of the flesh, the lust of the eyes, and the pride of life** are sin even though they feel good and satisfy something in us. God knows we have a fleshly, bodily nature, and physical needs that feel good when satisfied. Yet it is not in God's nature to influence us through the **lust of the flesh**.

i. God knows we have eyes, and that appearance means a lot to us. He made a beautiful world to please us! But God always looks beyond the outward appearance, and it is not in God's nature to influence us through the **lust of the eyes**.

ii. God knows we have emotional and psychological needs to be wanted and to accomplish things. He made us this way! But it is not in God's nature to influence us through **the pride of life**.

d. **Not of the Father but is of the world**: We often rarely appreciate how much the world dominates our thinking and how often our thoughts are more **of the world** than **of the Father**.

i. We usually believe that we think much more Biblically than we really do. We should rigorously measure our habits of thinking and see if they follow more **the world** or God our **Father**.

- Think of your standard for success: is it worldly or godly? Would you consider the apostle Paul a failure or a success?

- Think of your standard for what makes a person of the opposite sex appealing. Is it a worldly standard or a godly standard?

- Think of your standard for spirituality: is it worldly or godly? There is a worldly spirituality out there, and many people embrace it.

ii. This shows how great our need is to *not be conformed to this world, but be transformed by the renewing of your mind* (Romans 12:2).

3. (17) The folly of worldliness.

**And the world is passing away, and the lust of it; but he who does the will of God abides forever.**

a. **The world is passing away**: This reveals the folly of worldliness. What we invest into the world we invest into what cannot last because **the world is passing away**. As we saw with the example of the tower of Babel, the world *never* wins out against God, though by some appearances it does.

i. **The world is passing away**. It is not a prayer, not a wish, and not a spiritual sounding desire. It is a *fact*. **The world is passing away**, and we must live our lives and think our thoughts aware of this *fact*.

b. **The world is passing away**: This is powerfully illustrated by the life of Lot in Genesis chapters 13, 14, and 19. Lot attached himself to a true spiritual man, named Abraham. Yet he was selfish and chose for himself what seemed the most lucrative, without considering the spiritual implications of what he was doing. He became financially prosperous, but pitched his tent toward a wicked, worldly city - Sodom. After a while, he was sitting in the gates of the city as one of Sodom's civic leaders. He had worldly status, influence, wealth, and comfort. Yet, it was all taken away in a moment when the judgment of God came upon Sodom and Gomorrah. Lot put all his eggs in the wrong basket, and was burned by the fact that **the world is passing away**.

i. The ancient pharaohs were buried in the pyramids with all sorts of riches, which were thought to be of some use to them in the world to come. In the end, they were only of use to the grave robbers. The pharaohs could take none of their worldly stuff with them to the world beyond. No one drives through the gates of heaven with a moving van filled with the stuff of this world. It is true: **The world is passing away**.

c. **He who does the will of God abides forever**: This stands in strong contrast to the passing world. Because some things are *forever*, it is much wiser to invest our lives into that which cannot be lost: doing **the will of God**.

i. We are in regular contact with three eternal things: the Holy Spirit of God, the people around you, and the eternal words recorded in the book you hold. Time, attention, and expense put into those things pays *eternal* rewards.

D. An attack on our relationship with God: false religion.

1. (18-19) The danger of false religion: the spirit of Antichrist.

**Little children, it is the last hour; and as you have heard that the Antichrist is coming, even now many antichrists have come, by which we know that it is the last hour. They went out from us, but they were not of us; for if they had been of us, they would have continued with us; but *they went out* that they might be made manifest, that none of them were of us.**

a. **Little children, it is the last hour**: John lived in the constant expectancy of Jesus' return, regarding his time as **the last hour**. This is an expectancy that we should also have, knowing that the Lord's return can come at any time.

i. Seeing the nature of our times and what the Bible says about the end times, we should regard ourselves as being in the *last few minutes*.

b. **The Antichrist is coming**: John here refers to an individual who has captured the imagination of many people, including those who don't even know the Bible. Many are ignorant about this person called **the Antichrist**, except what they have learned from movies like *The Omen*.

i. The name **Antichrist** is important to understand. The prefix *anti* can mean "the opposite of" or "instead of." The **Antichrist** is the "opposite Jesus"; he is the "instead of" Jesus.

ii. Most people have focused on the idea of the "opposite Jesus." This has made them think that the Antichrist will appear as a *supremely evil* person. They think that as much as Jesus went around doing good, the Antichrist will go around doing bad. As much as Jesus' character and personality was beautiful and attractive, the Antichrist's character and personality will be ugly and repulsive. As much as Jesus spoke only truth, the Antichrist will speak only lies. This emphasizes the idea of the "opposite Jesus" too much. The Antichrist will instead be more of an "instead of Jesus." He will look wonderful, be charming and successful. He will be the ultimate winner, and appear as an angel of light.

iii. Some have wondered if this **Antichrist** will be an individual or a political system. This is really a small distinction, because it will in a sense be *both* a person and a political system. To a large extent, a man does represent and personify an entire government or system; when we think of Germany in the 1930s and 1940s, the figures of Hitler as an individual and Nazi Germany as a state are virtually the same. The Antichrist is an individual, but he will also be associated with a powerful government.

c. **The Antichrist is coming, even now many antichrists have come**: There is a distinction between **the Antichrist** and **many antichrists**. There is a "spirit" of antichrist, and this "spirit" of antichrist will one day find its ultimate fulfillment in *the* **Antichrist**, who will lead humanity in an end-times rebellion against God.

i. In other words, though the world still waits to see the ultimate revealing of the Antichrist, there are little "previews" of this man and his mission to come. These are the **antichrists** with a little "a" instead of a capital letter "A."

d. **By which we know that it is the last hour**: This indicates that John expected that the presence of **many antichrists** - of many people who offer a false, substitute Christ — is evidence of the lateness in the hour before Jesus' coming. John writes that this was true in his day; we could say it is even *truer* in our own.

i. "The word 'antichrist' occurs in the Bible only in the letters of John and that only five times in four verses (1 John 2:18, 22, 4:3; 2 John 7); but though the word is infrequent the idea of antichrist is frequent and is an important one." (Boice)

ii. This Antichrist goes by many titles:

- He is the *little horn* in Daniel 7:8.
- He is the *king of fierce countenance* in Daniel 8:23.
- He is the *Prince that shall come* in Daniel 9:26.
- He is the *willful king* in Daniel 11:36-45.
- He is the one who comes *in his own name* in John 5:43.
- He is the *son of perdition*, the *man of sin*, and the *lawless one* in 2 Thessalonians 2:3 and 2:8.

iii. Essentially, **the Antichrist** is a world dictator who leads humanity in what seems to be a golden age, until he shows his true colors - and the judgment of God is poured out on him and his empire immediately before the return of Jesus.

iv. We should take notice, because the world stage is set for a political and economic "superman" to arise, a single political leader to organize a world-dominating confederation of nations. National leaders speak of a new world order, but no one has been able to really define it, much less lead it. Yet this leader is coming.

v. This Antichrist will have surrounding him the kind of personality cult we are conditioned to accept today. Not only in America do we practice a sick worship of celebrities, but around the world, nations of hundreds of millions of people have been induced to worship a person - like Lenin, Stalin, or Mao. This shows us just how strong a personality cult can be when the government gets behind it whole-heartedly. All these developments should make us understand that the Antichrist is ready to be revealed when the moment is right.

e. **They went out from us**: This shows that many of these **antichrists** at one time or another identified themselves with Christian communities. The fact that they left the body of Christ demonstrated that they **were not of us** to begin with.

i. John wasn't talking about someone who leaves one church to begin attending another good church. He meant those who leave the community of God's people all together. This reveals that they were never really part of God's people to begin with.

ii. We can imagine the scene. There is some controversy among people at a church, and someone responds by saying, "I'm so sick of all this. This church and all churches, they're just a bunch of hypocrites. I don't need any of this. I can follow God my own way!" They leave; not just a church, but they leave any kind of church. We can fairly say that this person does not appear to be a Christian, and their appearance demonstrates that they never really were a Christian. Only God knows the heart for certain, but the appearance is that they trusted in the church, or trusted in themselves, but they weren't really trusting in Jesus Christ. If they were, then the common ground of trust in Jesus would be greater than any other difficulty they might be having with other Christians.

iii. One must beware of those who seem to be so "spiritual" that they can't get along in any church. One sees these from time to time: people who seem to be so gifted, so prophetic, or so spiritual that they get kicked out or leave in a huff from every church they go to. Finally, they are just left to themselves, and they seem happy enough with that. Fellowship with themselves is at least fellowship with someone as spiritual as they are! Of course, there is something seriously wrong with such so-called spirituality.

iv. "Perhaps most visible-church members are also members of the invisible church, the mystical body of Christ, but some are not. They are *with us* yet do *not really belong to us*. They share our earthly company but not our heavenly birth." (Stott)

v. The sobering truth is that many of those who offer a false or opposing Jesus came from the true body of Christians.

f. **They went out that they might be made manifest, that none of them were of us**: A healthy church can purge itself of poisons; the compromising and false Christian will not feel comfortable setting down roots in a healthy church - he will either get right with God or leave.

2. (20-23) Identifying the spirit of antichrist.

**But you have an anointing from the Holy One, and you know all things. I have not written to you because you do not know the truth, but because you know it, and that no lie is of the truth. Who is a liar but he who denies that Jesus is the Christ? He is antichrist who denies the Father and the Son. Whoever denies the Son does not have the Father either; he who acknowledges the Son has the Father also.**

a. **You have an anointing**: Here John refered to a common anointing, belonging to all believers. This is an anointing that makes discernment possible for those who seek it in the Lord (**and you know all things**).

i. When the New Testament speaks of **anointing**, it speaks of it as the common property of all believers. This is true even though all believers may not be walking in the anointing God has given them. The New Testament does not speak of a "special" anointing given to particular individuals.

ii. Among some Christians today, there is a rather magical or superstitious approach to this idea of **anointing**. In their mind, the anointing is like a virus or a germ that can be spread by casual contact or infect a whole group. Usually these folks think that when one "catches" the anointing, you can tell because they begin acting strangely. This isn't the Bible's idea of **anointing**.

iii. **Anointing** has the idea of being filled with and blessed by the Holy Spirit. This is something that is the common property of *all* Christians, but something we can and should become more submitted and responsive to. "As *oil* was used among the Asiatics for the inauguration of persons in important offices, and this oil was acknowledged to be an emblem of the *gifts* and *graces of the Holy Spirit*, without which the duties of those offices could not be discharged; so it is put here for the Spirit himself, who presided in the Church, and from which all gifts and graces flowed." (Clarke)

iv. This idea of **anointing** - literally, to be blessed with oil - was said to be the reason behind one of the punishments given to John in persecution. The Roman emperor Domitian cast John in a boiling vat of oil, as if to say, "Here is a real anointing." John emerged from the vat of boiling oil unharmed, because he was anointed indeed.

b. **And you know all things**: Because of the anointing of the Holy Spirit given to all believers, they possess the resources for knowing the truth. This isn't to say that teachers are unnecessary, because one of the resources for knowing the truth is the reminding given by teachers like John.

i. In verse 20, John used a different word for **know** than he mostly used before. Previously John used the word meaning *knowledge by experience*; here he used the word meaning *knowledge by intuition*. We know some things intuitively by the anointing of the Holy Spirit.

c. **Who is a liar but he who denies that Jesus is the Christ?** The context makes it clear that to affirm **that Jesus is the Christ** has to do with more than just saying, "He is the Messiah." It has to do with understanding the relationship between Jesus and God the Father: **He is antichrist who denies the Father and the Son**. In other words, someone could say, "I believe Jesus is the Christ . . . *as I define "Christ."* But we must believe that Jesus is the Christ, the Messiah, as the Bible defines **Christ** - the Messiah, who is fully God and fully man; who perfectly revealed the Father to us.

d. **He is antichrist who denies the Father and the Son**: The spirit of antichrist identifies itself by its denial of Jesus and its denial of the Father, remembering that Jesus and the Father can be denied even by those who seem to speak well of them both.

i. We can deny Jesus while praising Him with our words; we can deny Him by offering a substitute Jesus or by ministering in a manner that denies the character of Jesus.

e. **Whoever denies the Son does not have the Father either**: John here repeated an idea that Jesus expressed often, as recorded in the Gospel of John. Jesus said, *He who believes in Me, believes not in Me but in Him who sent Me. And he who sees Me sees Him who sent Me* (John 12:44-45). *He who receives Me receives Him who sent Me* (John 13:20).

i. Often times it is said, "We all worship the same God. You have one name for Him and I have another. But that doesn't matter. We are just talking about different roads to the same God because we all have the same God." Here is the question to ask in response: "Was your God perfectly revealed in Jesus Christ?" If your God was, then you have the same God. If your God wasn't perfectly revealed in Jesus, then you do not have the same God as in the Bible.

ii. There are many people who seem rather spiritual or religious, yet reject Jesus Christ. While their religion or spirituality may do them much good in this life - giving them a basis for morality and good behavior - it does them nothing before God, because in rejecting Jesus they reject God.

E. Abiding: preserving our relationship.

1. (24) Preserving relationship against the threat of the spirit of antichrist: abiding in the true Christian message and abiding in God.

**Therefore let that abide in you which you heard from the beginning. If what you heard from the beginning abides in you, you also will abide in the Son and in the Father.**

a. **Therefore**: In light of the danger of the spirit of antichrist, we protect ourselves against the spirit of antichrist by abiding in the original, core Christian message (that **which you heard from the beginning**). As we walk in the simplicity and power of that message, we will not be led astray.

i. Humans, by nature, are almost always attracted to something just because it is *new*. We almost always think of *new* as *better*. But when it comes to *truth*, new is not better. That **which you heard from the beginning** is better.

ii. The apostle Paul communicated the same idea in Galatians 1:6-9, where he warns against going after a new gospel and emphasizes the importance of continuing on in the original gospel that Paul taught.

iii. This is difficult because we are tempted to be *tossed to and fro and carried about with every wind of doctrine, by the trickery of men, in the cunning craftiness of deceitful plotting* (Ephesians 4:14). We often itch for something "new" and "exciting" even if it departs from that **which you heard from the beginning**.

b. **Which you heard from the beginning**: This does not describe whatever teaching any Christian might receive when he is newly following Jesus. **The beginning**, for these believers, describes the time when they were under the teaching of the apostles, which is now recorded for us in the New Testament.

i. Simply put, we **abide in** what is **from the beginning** when we stay close to our Bibles. If that was your environment when you were a young Christian, wonderful. But if it was not, then put yourself in that environment now.

c. **Let that abide in you**: This doesn't mean just knowing it, but *living* in it. When we are living in the simplicity of the truth of Jesus Christ, then we will **abide in the Son and in the Father**.

i. Our world is filled with people searching for God, some sincerely and some insincerely. But if someone wants to really *live in God*, John tells us how: let the message of the apostles (**which you heard from the beginning**) live in you.

ii. John did *not* say, "If you *know* God's Word, you *know* God," because someone can have a bare, intellectual knowledge of God's Word. But he *did* say, "If God's Word *lives* in you, *God* lives in you." We can come to a living, growing, relationship with God through His Word.

d. **You also will abide in the Son and in the Father**: This is absolutely necessary for the Christian life. John will use the word **abide** six times in these few verses, and the idea is repeated throughout the New Testament.

i. Abiding in Jesus (*living* in Jesus) is not a passive thing; it is an *active* thing. We must give ourselves both mentally and spiritually to living in Jesus. "We abide in him, not by a physical law, as a mass of iron abides on the earth; but by a mental and spiritual law, by which the greatness of divine love and goodness holds us fast to the Lord Jesus." (Spurgeon)

ii. Yet, not only are we called to abide in Him; but we also know that He abides in us. It is a two-way relationship. "You are to take care that you abide in Christ as much as if all depended upon yourself; and yet you can look to the promise of the covenant, and see that the real reason for your abiding in Christ lies in the operation of his unchanging love and grace." (Spurgeon)

2. (25) The blessing of abiding in the truth and in God: eternal life.

**And this is the promise that He has promised us; eternal life.**

a. **This is the promise**: When His truth (what we *heard from the beginning*) lives in us, then God lives in us. When God lives in us, we have a **promise**. In this kind of life, the promise of **eternal life** is real.

b. **Eternal life**: This is not mere immortality. Every human being, made in the image of God, is immortal, in the sense that our souls will live *forever*, either in heaven or in hell. So, **eternal life** doesn't just mean a life that lasts for eternity. It describes the kind of life that God, the *Eternal One*, has in Himself.

i. Therefore, while the idea of **eternal life** has reference to the life beyond this present world, it doesn't begin when we die. If we don't have **eternal life** now, we won't get it when we die.

ii. This is why it is so important to have the **promise** of eternal life right now. And we have this **promise** if God's truth *abides in you*, and we *abide in the Son and in the Father*.

iii. So, abiding is our grounds of confidence with God. We have the **promise** of eternal life as we abide. "You must be in a living, loving, lasting union with the Son of God, or else you are not in a state of salvation." (Spurgeon)

3. (26-27) Our protection against deception: **the anointing**.

**These things I have written to you concerning those who *try to* deceive you. But the anointing which you have received from Him abides in you, and you do not need that anyone teach you; but as the same anointing teaches you concerning all things, and is true, and is not a lie, and just as it has taught you, you will abide in Him.**

a. **These things I have written**: John knew there was deception among these early Christians, and it concerned him. He had a passion to keep them consistent with God's message of truth.

b. **The anointing which you have received from Him abides in you**: This abiding and anointing is what enables Christians to continue in the truth.

i. John first referred to this **anointing** back in 1 John 2:20. This **anointing** is not the private property of a few special or spectacular Christians. All Christians have the presence of God's Spirit within them.

c. **You do not need that anyone teach you**: Just as he stated in 1 John 2:20 (*you know all things*), John tells us again that the anointing we receive from God guides us into truth. We are guided into truth on a one-on-one level, God confirming it to our hearts.

i. Again, John's message is simple. Because of the anointing of the Holy Spirit given to all believers, they possess the resources for knowing the truth. This is not to say that teachers are unnecessary, because one of the resources for knowing the truth is the reminder given by teachers like John.

d. **You will abide in Him**: This anointing which guides us into truth will also guide us closer to Jesus.

4. (28-29) What it means to live in Jesus.

**And now, little children, abide in Him, that when He appears, we may have confidence and not be ashamed before Him at His coming. If you know that He is righteous, you know that everyone who practices righteousness is born of Him.**

a. **Abide in Him, that when He appears, we may have confidence and not be ashamed**: Abiding in Jesus means that we need not be afraid or **ashamed** when Jesus returns. This is because we have intimately known Him, and therefore we can have **confidence** at His coming.

i. John brings up a challenging image. When Jesus returns, some people will be afraid because they never knew Jesus at all. But among those who know Him, some will not be afraid, they will be **ashamed before Him at His coming**. They will realize that they have been living worldly, unfruitful lives. In one moment, the understanding will overwhelm them that whatever else they accomplished in life, they did not **abide in Him** as they could have.

ii. Paul the Apostle speaks of those who are "barely saved": *he will suffer loss; but he himself will be saved, yet so as through fire* (1 Corinthians 3:15). There are those who, for at least a moment, the coming of Jesus will be a moment of disappointment rather than glory.

iii. It is important for us to carefully consider these matters because it is difficult to measure the distance between "barely saved" and "almost saved." It is dangerous to contemplate questions such as, "How little can I do and still make it to heaven?" or "How far can I stray from the Shepherd and still be part of the flock?" Instead we should be diligent to not be **ashamed before Him at His coming**.

iv. "What is the way to prepare for Christ's coming? By the study of the prophecies? Yes, if you are sufficiently instructed to be able to understand them. 'To be prepared for the Lord's coming,' some enthusiasts might say, 'had I not better spend a month in retirement, and get out of this wicked world?' You may, if you like; and especially you will do so if you are lazy. But the one Scriptural prescription for preparing for his coming is this, 'Abide in him.' If you abide in the faith of him, holding his truth, following his example, and making him your dwelling-place, your Lord may come at any hour, and you will welcome him." (Spurgeon)

b. **When He appears, we may have confidence and not be ashamed**: We never grow beyond our need to abide and find our confidence in abiding in Jesus. Because John used "**we**" instead of "you," we know that *he* needed this confidence also.

c. **Abide in Him**: This is the way to be confident when Jesus comes. When you **abide in Him**, you are ready for Jesus to come at any time.

i. The idea of living in Jesus is so important in the Bible. Jesus promised in John 14:23: *If anyone loves Me, he will keep My word; and My Father will love him, and We will come to him and make Our home with him.*

ii. Paul expressed this idea in his prayer for the Ephesians in Ephesians 3:17: *that Christ may dwell in your hearts through faith*. There are two Greek words to convey the idea of "to live in"; one has the idea of living in a place as a stranger, and the other has the idea of settling down in a place to make it your permanent home. *Dwell* in Ephesians 3:17 uses the ancient Greek word for a permanent home, indicating that Jesus wants to settle down in your heart, not just visit as a stranger.

iii. Do you **abide in Him**? Or do you just visit Jesus every once in a while? Abiding in Jesus gives us **confidence** because we know we wouldn't change our lives substantially if we somehow knew Jesus would come back next week. We would already be abiding in Him.

**d. Everyone who practices righteousness is born of Him**: Abiding in Jesus means that we will practice righteousness in our lives because we are **born of Him**. Being born again has changed our lives from a disposition to sin to a disposition to righteousness.

i. This is a *test* of our abiding in Him, the same kind of test John mentioned in 1 John 1:6, 2:4, and 2:9. There is something wrong if someone claims to be **born of Him** and he does not **practice righteousness**.

ii. When someone is born of someone else, there is almost always a family resemblance. You say, "Look, she has her mother's eyes" or "He has his father's nose." Well, the children of God have a family resemblance to their Father in heaven. **He is righteous**, so those who are **born of Him** also **practice righteousness**. "God hath no children destitute of his image, or who resemble him not." (Poole)

iii. We will not *perfect* righteousness until we are glorified with Jesus; but we can *practice* righteousness right now, as we are **born of Him**.

iv. There are three precious claims for each Christian in this chapter. *I know Him* (1 John 2:4), *I abide in Him* (1 John 2:6), and I am *in the light* (1 John 2:9). John wants us to know that if these statements are true, it will show in our lives, especially in our love for brothers and sisters in Jesus.

# 1 John 3 - The Love of God and the Life of Love

A. The destiny of our relationship with God.

1. (1) The glory of God's love.

**Behold what manner of love the Father has bestowed on us, that we should be called children of God! Therefore the world does not know us, because it did not know Him.**

a. **Behold what manner of love the Father has bestowed on us, that we should be called children of God!** Having just mentioned being *born of Him*, John speaks in amazement about this **manner of love** that makes us **children of God**. He wants us to **behold it** - that is, look at it and study it intently.

i. It is of great benefit to the Christian to take a good, intense look at the love of God **bestowed on us**.

ii. **Bestowed on us** speaks many things. First, it speaks of the *measure* of God's love to us; it could more literally be translated *lavished on us*. Secondly, it speaks of the *manner* of God's giving of love; **bestowed** has the idea of a one-sided giving, instead of a return for something earned. What is my role if God is to

iii. What is it that makes us slow to believe the love of God? Sometimes it is *pride*, which demands to prove itself worthy of the love of God before it will receive it. Sometimes it is *unbelief*, which cannot trust the love of God when it sees the hurt and pain of life. And sometimes it just takes *time* for a person to come to a fuller understanding of the greatness of God's love.

iv. **Behold** means that God wants to *see* this love and He is not ashamed to show it to us. " 'There,' he says, 'you poor people that love me you sick people, you unknown, obscure people, without any talent, I have published it before heaven and earth, and made the angels know it, that you are my children, and I am not ashamed of you. I glory in the fact that I have taken you for my sons and daughters.' " (Spurgeon)

b. **That we should be called children of God**: The greatness of this love is shown in that by it, we are **called children of God**. As God looked down on lost humanity, He might have merely had a charitable compassion, a pity on our plight, both in this life and in eternity. With a mere pity, He might have set forth a plan of salvation where man could be saved from hell. But God went far beyond that, to call us the **children of God**.

i. Who calls us the children of God?

- The Father does (*"I will be a Father to you, and you shall be My sons and daughters, says the LORD Almighty,"* 2 Corinthians 6:18)

- The Son does (*He is not ashamed to call them brethren,* Hebrews 2:11)

- The Spirit does (*The Spirit Himself bears witness with our spirit that we are children of God,* Romans 8:16)

ii. There is a sense in which this is a totally "unnecessary" blessing that God gives in the course of salvation, and a demonstration of His true and deep love for us. We can picture someone helping or saving someone, but not going so far as to make them a part of the family - but this is what God has done for us.

iii. In this, we gain something in Jesus Christ greater than Adam ever possessed. We never once read of Adam being called one of the **children of God** in the sense John means here. He was never adopted as a son of God in the way believers are. We err when we think of redemption as merely a restoration of what was lost with Adam; we are granted more in Jesus than Adam ever had.

iv. If we are truly **children of God**, then it should show in our likeness to our Father and in our love for our "siblings."

v. It is important to understand what it means to be the **children of God**, and that everyone is not a child of God in the sense John meant it here. God's love is expressed to all in the giving of Jesus for the sins of the world (John 3:16), but this does not make all of humanity the **children of God** in the sense John means it here. Here he speaks of those who have *received* the love of Jesus in a life of fellowship and trust with Him; *But as many as received Him, to them He gave the right to become children of God, to those who believe in His name* (John 1:12).

c. **Therefore the world does not know us**: Because of our unique parentage from God, we are strangers to this world (or should be).

i. This shows the great danger of a Christianity that works so hard to show the world just how much like the world they can be; we can not be surprised or offended to find out that **the world does not know us**.

d. **Because it did not know Him**: Ultimately, we should expect the world to treat us as it treated **Him** - rejecting Jesus and crucifying Jesus. While it is true that Jesus loved sinners and they, recognizing that love, flocked to Him, we must also remember that it was the world that cried out *crucify Him!*

2. (2) The destiny of God's children.

**Beloved, now we are children of God; and it has not yet been revealed what we shall be, but we know that when He is revealed, we shall be like Him, for we shall see Him as He is.**

a. **Now we are children of God**: Our present standing is plain. We can know, and have an assurance, that we are indeed among the **children of God**. Romans 8:16 tells us, *The Spirit Himself bears witness with our spirit that we are children of God.* If you are a child of God, you have an inward assurance of this.

b. **It has not yet been revealed what we shall be**: Though our present standing is plain, our future destiny is clouded. We don't know in the kind of detail we would like to know what we will become in the world beyond. In this sense, we can't even imagine what we will be like in glory.

i. "What we are does not now appear to the world; what we shall be does not yet appear to us." (Stott)

ii. "If I may use such an expression, *this is not the time for the manifestation of a Christian's glory.* Eternity is to be the period for the Christian's full development, and for the sinless display of his God-given glory. Here, he must expect to be unknown; it is in the hereafter that he is to be discovered as a son of the great King." (Spurgeon)

c. **We know that when He is revealed, we shall be like Him, for we shall see Him as He is**: We are not left completely in the dark about our future state. When Jesus is revealed to us, either by His coming for us or our coming to Him, **we shall be like Him**.

i. The Bible speaks of God's great plan for our lives like this: *For whom He foreknew, He also predestined to be conformed to the image of His Son, that He might be the firstborn among many brethren* (Romans 8:29). God's ultimate goal in our lives is to make us like Jesus, and here, John speaks of the fulfillment of that purpose.

ii. This does not mean that we cease to be ourselves, full of the distinct personality and character God has given us. Heaven will not be like the Nirvana of Eastern mysticism, where all personality is dissolved into God like a drop into the ocean. We will still be ourselves, but our character and nature will be perfected into the image of Jesus' perfection. We will not be "clones" of Jesus in heaven!

iii. The Christian should long to be like Jesus, yet remember that God will never force a person to be like Jesus if he doesn't want to. And that is what hell is for: people who don't want to be like Jesus. The sobering, eternal truth is this: God gives man what he really wants. If you really want to be like Jesus, it will show in your life now, and it will be a fact in eternity. If you don't really want to be like Jesus, it will also show in your life now, and it will also be a fact in eternity.

iv. **We *shall be* like Him**: This reminds us that even though we grow into the image of Jesus now, we still have a long way to go. None of us will be finished until we see Jesus, and only then truly **we shall be like Him**.

d. **We shall see Him as He is**: Perhaps this is the greatest glory of heaven: not to be personally glorified, but to be in the unhindered, unrestricted, presence of our Lord.

i. Paul said of our present walk, *For now we see in a mirror, dimly, but then face to face. Now I know in part, but then I shall know just as I also am known* (1 Corinthians 13:12). Today, when we look in a good mirror, the image is clear. But in the ancient world, mirrors were made out of polished metal, and the image was always unclear and somewhat distorted. We see Jesus now only in a dim, unclear way, but one day we will see Him with perfect clarity.

ii. Heaven is precious to us for many reasons. We long to be with loved ones who have passed before us and whom we miss so dearly. We long to be with the great men and women of God who have passed before us in centuries past. We want to walk the streets of gold, see the pearly gates, and see the angels round the throne of God worshipping Him day and night. However, none of those things, precious as they are, make heaven really "heaven." What makes heaven, heaven, is the unhindered, unrestricted, presence of our Lord, and to **see Him as He is** will be the greatest experience of our eternal existence.

iii. What will we see when we see Jesus? Revelation 1:13-16 describes a vision of Jesus in heaven: *He was dressed in a long robe with a golden* [breastplate]*; His head and His hair were white as snow-white wool, His eyes blazed* *like fire, and His feet shone as the finest bronze glows in the furnace. His voice had the sound of a great waterfall, and I saw that in His right hand He held seven stars. A sharp two-edged sword came out of His mouth, and His face was ablaze like the sun at its height.* (J.B. Phillips translation) This isn't the same Jesus who walked this earth, looking like a normal man.

iv. At the same time, we know that in heaven, Jesus will still bear the scars of His suffering on this earth. After Jesus rose from the dead in His glorified body, His body uniquely retained the nail prints in His hands and the scar on his side (John 20:24-29). In Zechariah 12:10, Jesus speaks prophetically of the day when the Jewish people, turned to Him, see Him in glory: *then they will look on Me whom they pierced. Yes, they will mourn for Him as one mourns for his only son, and grieve for Him as one grieves for a firstborn.* Zechariah 13:6 continues the thought: *And one will say to him, "What are these wounds between your arms?" Then he will answer, "Those with which I was wounded in the house of my friends."*

e. **We shall be like Him, for we shall see Him as He is**: John made the connection between seeing **Him as He is** and our transformation to be like Jesus. We can say that the same principle is at work right now. To the extent that you see Jesus **as He is**, to that same extent, you are like Him in your life.

i. We can say that this happens by *reflection*. "When a man looks into a bright mirror, it makes him also bright, for it throws its own light upon his face; and, in a much more wonderful fashion, when we look at Christ, who is all brightness, he throws some of his brightness upon us." (Spurgeon)

3. (3) Knowing our destiny purifies our lives right now.

**And everyone who has this hope in Him purifies himself, just as He is pure.**

a. **Everyone who has this hope in Him purifies himself**: Knowing our eternal destiny, and living in **this hope** will purify our lives. When we know our end is to be more like Jesus, it makes us want to be more like Jesus right now.

i. Having the anticipation of being with Jesus, of the soon coming of Jesus Christ, can have a marvelous purifying effect in our lives. It makes us want to be ready, to be serving Him now, to be pleasing Him now.

b. **This hope in Him**: Ultimately, our hope is not in heaven or in our own glory in heaven. Our hope is **in Him**. We must never set our hope on other things; not on a relationship, on success, on mutual fund, on your health, on your possessions, or simply just on our self. Our only real hope is **in Him**.

B. Sin: An Attack on Relationship.

1. (4-5) The nature of sin and Jesus' work in removing our sin.

**Whoever commits sin also commits lawlessness, and sin is lawlessness. And you know that He was manifested to take away our sins, and in Him there is no sin.**

a. **Sin is lawlessness**: John defines sin at its most basic root. It is a disregard for the law of God, which is inherently a disregard for the law *Maker*, God Himself.

> i. We often fail in the battle against sin because we won't call it for what it is: lawlessness, an offense against the Great Law Maker, God. Instead, we say things like "If I've done anything wrong . . ." or "Mistakes were made . . ." and so forth. Call it for what it is: sin and lawlessness. "The first step towards holy living is to recognize the true nature and wickedness of sin." (Stott)

b. **You know that He was manifested to take away our sins**: John here defined the mission of Jesus Christ at its most basic root - **to take away our sins**. The angel Gabriel promised Joseph regarding the ministry of Jesus: *you shall call His name JESUS, for He shall save His people from their sin* (Matthew 1:21).

> i. Jesus takes away our sin in the sense of taking the *penalty* of our sin. This is immediately accomplished when one comes by faith to Jesus.

> ii. Jesus takes away our sin in the sense of taking the *power* of sin away. This is an ongoing work in the lives of those who walk after Jesus.

> iii. Jesus takes away our sin in the sense of taking the *presence* of sin away. This is a work that will be completed when we pass into eternity and are glorified with Jesus.

c. **He was manifested to take away our sins**: This is the work of Jesus in our life. It is a work we must respond to, but it is *His* work in us.

> i. We cannot **take away** the *penalty* of our own sin. It is impossible to cleanse ourselves in this way. We must instead receive the work of Jesus in taking away our sin.

> ii. We cannot **take away** the *power* of sin in our lives. This is His work in us, and we respond to that work. Someone who comes to Jesus does not have to clean himself up first, but he must be willing to have Him **take away** his sin.

> iii. We cannot **take away** the *presence* of sin in our lives. This is His work in us, ultimately accomplished when we will be glorified with Him.

d. **In Him there is no sin**: Jesus had no sin to take away; therefore, He could take away our sin, taking it upon Himself.

2. (6) Abiding in sin or abiding in God.

**Whoever abides in Him does not sin. Whoever sins has neither seen Him nor known Him.**

a. **Whoever abides in Him does not sin**: Since *sin is lawlessness*, a disregard for God (1 John 3:4), and since Jesus came *to take away our sins* (1 John 3:5), and since in Jesus *there is no sin* (1 John 3:5), then to **abide in Him** means to **not sin**.

i. It is very important to understand what the Bible means - and what it does not mean - when it says **does not sin**. According to the verb tense John uses, **does not sin** means *does not live a life style of habitual sin*. John has already told us in 1 John 1:8 *If we say we have no sin, we deceive ourselves, and the truth is not in us*. In 1 John 1:8, the grammar indicates John is speaking about occasional acts of sin. The grammar of 1 John 3:6 indicates that John is speaking of a settled, continued lifestyle of sin. John is not teaching here the possibility of sinless perfection.

ii. "The present tense in the Greek verb implied habit, continuity, unbroken sequence" (Stott); the NIV has the right idea when it translates these verbs with phrases such as *keeps on sinning, continues to sin*, and *he cannot go on sinning*.

b. **Whoever abides in Him does not sin**: John's message is plain and consistent with the rest of the Scriptures. It tells us that a life style of habitual sin is inconsistent with a life of abiding in Jesus Christ. A true Christian can only be *temporarily* in a life style of sin.

i. Paul's teaching in Romans 6 is a great example of this principle. He shows us that when a person comes to Jesus, when his sins are forgiven and God's grace is extended to him, he is radically changed - the old man is dead, and the new man lives. So it is utterly incompatible for a new creation in Christ to be comfortable in habitual sin; such a place can only be temporary for the Christian.

ii. In some ways, the question is not "Do you sin or not?" We each sin. The question is, "How do you react when you sin? Do you give into the pattern of sin, and let it dominate your lifestyle? Or do you humbly confess your sin, and do battle against it with the power Jesus can give?"

iii. This is why it is so grieving to see Christians make excuses for their sin, and not humbly confess them. Unless the sin is dealt with squarely, it will contribute to a pattern of sin that may soon become their lifestyle - perhaps a secret lifestyle, but a lifestyle nonetheless.

iv. What is important is that we never sign a "peace treaty" with sin. We never wink at its presence or excuse it by saying, "Everybody has his own sinful areas, and this is mine. Jesus understands." This completely goes against everything we are in Jesus, and the work He has done in our life.

c. **Whoever sins has neither seen Him nor known Him**: To live a lifestyle of habitual sin is to demonstrate that you have not **seen Him** (in a present sense of the ultimate "seeing Him mentioned in 1 John 3:2), and that you have not **known Him**. There are some people so great and so wonderful that seeing them or knowing them will change your life forever. Jesus is that kind of person.

3. (7) Righteousness will show in a person's life.

**Little children, let no one deceive you. He who practices righteousness is righteous, just as He is righteous.**

a. **Let no one deceive you**: This tells us that John wrote against a deception threatening the Christians of his day.

b. **He who practices righteousness is righteous**: John did not allow us to separate a *religious* righteousness from a life of righteousness. If we are made righteous by our faith in Jesus Christ (Romans 3:22), it will be seen by our righteous lives.

i. The most important thing a person can ever do is make sure he is **righteous** before God. This simply means he is held in *right standing* before God. It's more than saying, "not guilty." It is more like saying, "Not guilty and in right standing." It speaks of the presence of good, not just the absence of evil.

ii. John is *not* saying that we are made righteous before God by our own righteous acts - the Bible clearly teaches that we are made righteous through faith in Jesus Christ - yet that righteousness in Jesus will be evident in our lives.

iii. Apparently, there were those who taught that you could be righteous before God with no evidence of righteousness in your life - John is rebuking this idea. Charles Spurgeon said it well: "The grace that does not change my life will not save my soul."

c. **Just as He is righteous**: We can live lives characterized by **righteousness**, not sin, because we have been given the righteousness of Jesus, and **He is righteous**. We have the resource we need to live righteously!

4. (8-9) The root of sin and the root of righteousness.

**He who sins is of the devil, for the devil has sinned from the beginning. For this purpose the Son of God was manifested, that He might destroy**

the works of the devil. **Whoever has been born of God does not sin, for His seed remains in him; and he cannot sin, because he has been born of God.**

a. **He who sins is of the devil**: People who are settled in habitual sin are not the children of God - they are **of the devil**, and Jesus came to destroy the works of the devil and free us from our bondage to the devil.

> i. "Well, labor under no mistake, sir. 'He that committeth sin is of the devil.' It is no use making excuses and apologies; if you are a lover of sin, you shall go where sinners go. If you, who live after this fashion, say that you have believed in the precious blood of Christ, I do not believe you, sir. If you had a true faith in that precious blood, you would hate sin. If you dare to say you are trusting in the atonement while you live in sin, you lie, sir; you do not trust in the atonement; for where there is a real faith in the atoning sacrifice, it purifies the man, and makes him hate the sin which shed the Redeemer's blood." (Spurgeon)

b. **For this purpose the Son of God was manifested, that He might destroy the works of the devil**: John gave us one reason why Jesus came in 1 John 3:5 (*He was manifested to take away our sins*). Now, John gives us another reason: **that He might destroy the works of the devil**.

> i. We can just imagine the heart of God grieving over the destruction the devil has wrought over this earth, and grieving that man has allowed the devil to do it all. Jesus came to put a stop to all that by overcoming the devil completely by His life, His suffering, His death, and His resurrection.

> ii. Note the purpose of Jesus: to **destroy the works of the devil**. Not to neutralize them, not to alleviate them, or not to limit them. Jesus wants to **destroy** the works of the devil!

> iii. Many people are unnecessarily afraid of the devil, fearing what he could do against them. If they only knew that as we walk in Jesus, the devil is afraid of us! As we walk in Jesus, we help in seeing Him **destroy the works of the devil!**

c. **Whoever has been born of God does not sin, for His seed remains in him**: The change from being **of the devil** to being **children of God** comes as we are **born of God**; when this happens, our old nature, patterned after the instinctive rebellion of Adam, dies - and we are given a new nature, patterned after the instinctive obedience of Jesus Christ.

> i. John here is simply emphasizing what it means to be *born again*. It means that a *change* comes into our lives - it is a change that will be

worked out into every area of our lives as we grow in Christ, but it is a real, observable change.

> ii. It is the same message Paul preached, saying that as believers we are to *put off, concerning your former conduct, the old man which grows corrupt according to the deceitful lusts*, and that we are to *put on the new man which was created according to God, in true righteousness and holiness* (Ephesians 4:22, 24).

d. **Does not sin . . . he cannot sin: Does not sin** and **cannot sin** each has the same verb tense as *does not sin* in 1 John 3:6, meaning a continual practice of habitual sin. John tells us that when we are born again - born into the family of God - there is a real change in our relation to sin.

## C. Hatred: An Attack on Relationship.

1. (10) Two essentials: righteous conduct and love for the brethren.

**In this the children of God and the children of the devil are manifest: Whoever does not practice righteousness is not of God, nor *is* he who does not love his brother.**

X

a. **The children of God and the children of the devil:** John has already introduced the idea of being a child of God (1 John 3:1, *that we should be called the children of God* and 1 John 3:9, *born of God*). He has already written of some being *of the devil* (1 John 3:8). But here, he makes it plain: some are **children of God** and some are **children of the devil**.

> i. John doesn't spend time trying to prove or explain the existence of the devil. He knows the reality of the devil is a Biblical fact. Some today lack John's wisdom and either deny the devil's existence or they are obsessed with the devil.

> ii. Some might think John is far too harsh in saying some are **children of the devil**, supposing perhaps that John did not love people as Jesus did. But Jesus called people **children of the devil** also in John 8:41-45. In this passage, Jesus' point was important, establishing the principle that our spiritual parentage determines our nature and our destiny. If we are born again, and have God as our Father, it will show in our nature and destiny. But whether our father is Satan or Adam, it will also show in our nature and destiny - just as it showed in these adversaries of Jesus.

b. **Are manifest:** John gave a simple - though not easy - way to identify who the **children of God and the children of the devil** are. **Whoever does not practice righteousness is not of God, nor is he who does not love his brother.**

i. Both of these are essential. Righteousness without love makes one a religious Pharisee, and love without righteousness makes one a partner in evil.

ii. How do righteousness and love "balance"? They don't. We are never to love at the expense of righteousness, and are never to be righteous at the expense of love. We aren't looking for a balance between the two, because they are not opposites. Real love is the greatest righteousness, and real righteousness is the greatest love.

iii. Love and righteousness are each most perfectly displayed in the nature of Jesus. He was both righteous, and completely loving.

**2. (11) The need to love one another.**

**For this is the message that you heard from the beginning, that we should love one another.**

a. **This is the message that you heard from the beginning**: John had already emphasized the command to love as being *the word which you heard from the beginning* (1 John 2:7). In remembering this message to **love one another**, he remembered the command of Jesus in John 13:34.

b. **That we should love one another**: The basic Christian message has not changed. Perhaps some have thought that because Christians talk about a "personal relationship with Jesus Christ" that it is only us and Jesus who matter. But how we treat others - how we **love one another** - really matters before God.

**3. (12) An example of hatred: Cain.**

**Not as Cain *who* was of the wicked one and murdered his brother. And why did he murder him? Because his works were evil and his brother's righteous.**

a. **Not as Cain**: As a negative example, John presents Cain, who was not right with God (**his works were evil**) and who hated his brother. When there are two children of God who are both right with God, there *will* be love.

b. **Who was of the wicked one**: Cain is a good example of the failure to love.

i. We can presume that Cain had a godly upbringing that should have equipped him to love, but he chose not to.

ii. Cain's disobedience came from a lack of faith (Hebrews 11:4) which resulted in first disobedience, then hatred.

iii. Cain's disobedience and hatred was based in pride (Genesis 4:5).

iv. Cain's disobedience and hatred made him miserable (Genesis 4:5).

v. Cain refused the warning God gave him, and gave into the sin of hatred (Genesis 4:6-7).

vi. Cain's sin of hatred led to action against the one he hated (Genesis 4:8).

vii. Cain was evasive about his sin of hatred, and tried to hide it. But God found him out (Genesis 4:9).

4. (13-15) Love as the evidence of the new birth.

**Do not marvel, my brethren, if the world hates you. We know that we have passed from death to life, because we love the brethren. He who does not love *his* brother abides in death. Whoever hates his brother is a murderer, and you know that no murderer has eternal life abiding in him.**

a. **Do not marvel**: We shouldn't be surprised when the world hates us; but we should be surprised when there is hatred among the body of Christ.

b. **We know**: John insists that the believer can come to a place of genuine assurance. "I have, heard it said, by those who would be thought philosophers, that in religion we must believe, but cannot know. I am not very clear about the distinction they draw between knowledge and faith, nor do I care to enquire; because I assert that, in matters relating to religion, we *know*; in the things of God, we both believe and know." (Spurgeon)

c. **We know that we have passed from death to life**: A love for the people of God is a basic sign of being born again. If this love is not evident in our lives, our salvation can be questioned. If it is present, it gives us assurance.

i. We can know we have **passed from death to life** by our love for other Christians. The place of hatred, of jealousy, of bitterness you find yourself in is a place of **death**. You need to pass **from death** over **to life**.

ii. This means knowing two things. First, **we know** that we were dead. Second, **we know** that we have passed to life from death. To pass **from death to life** is the reverse of the normal. We all expect to pass from life to death; but in Jesus, we can turn it around.

iii. This speaks to our pursuit of fellowship. If we love the brethren, we will want to be with them - and even if we have been battered and bruised by unloving brethren, there will still be something in us drawing us back to fellowship with the brethren we love.

iv. "Do you love them *for Christ's sake?* Do you say to yourself, 'That is one of Christ's people; that is one who bears Christ's cross; that is one of the children of God; therefore I love him, and take delight in his company'? Then, that is an evidence that you are not of the world." (Spurgeon)

d. **Whoever hates his brother is a murderer**: To hate our brother is to murder him in our hearts. Though we may not carry out the action (through cowardice or fear of punishment), we *wish* that person dead. Or, by ignoring another person, we may *treat* them as if they were dead. Hatred can be shown *passively* or *actively*.

> i. John seemed to have in mind the teaching of Jesus from the Sermon on the Mount regarding the true fulfillment of the law (Matthew 5:21-22).

> ii. "In the heart there is no difference; to hate is to despise, to cut off from relationship, and murder is simply the fulfillment of that attitude." (Barker)

> iii. "Every man who hates another has the venom of murder in his veins. He may never actually take the deadly weapons into his hand and destroy life; but if he wishes that his brother were out of the way, if he would be glad if no such person existed, that feeling amounts to murder in the judgment of God." (Spurgeon)

e. **You know that no murderer has eternal life abiding in him**: To live in the practice of murder - or to have a life style of the habitual hatred of our brethren - is a demonstration that we do not have **eternal life abiding in** us, that we are not born again.

> i. There are many people for whom being a Christian is a "none of the above" sort of thing. They consider themselves Christians because they are not Moslems, or Jewish, or Buddhists, or atheists. But being a Christian is never a "none of the above" kind of thing.

> ii. Being a Christian is more than saying, "I am a Christian." There are in fact some who claim to be Christians who are not. How can we know if we are one of these? John's reply has been constant and simple. There are three tests to measure the proof of a genuine Christian: the truth test, the love test, and the moral test. If we believe in what the Bible teaches as true, if we show the love of Jesus to others, and if our conduct has been changed and is becoming more like Jesus, then our claim to be a Christian can be proven true.

D. What love is and how we should love one another.

1. (16) The objective reality of love and how it shows in our life.

**By this we know love, because He laid down His life for us. And we also ought to lay down *our* lives for the brethren.**

a. **By this we know love**: What is love? How we define love is important. If we define love the wrong way, then everyone passes, or no one passes, the love test. To understand the Biblical idea of love, we should begin by understanding the vocabulary of love among the ancient Greeks, who gave us the original language of the New Testament.

i. *Eros* was one word for love. It described, as we might guess from the word itself, *erotic* love. It referred to sexual love.

ii. *Storge* was the second word for love. It referred to family love, the kind of love there is between a parent and child, or between family members in general.

iii. *Philia* is the third word for love. It spoke of a brotherly friendship and affection. It is the love of deep friendship and partnership. *Philia* love might be described as the highest love that one is capable of without God's help.

iv. *Agape* is the fourth word for love. It described a love that loves without changing. It is a self-giving love that gives without demanding or expecting re-payment. It is love so great that it can be given to the unlovable or unappealing. It is love that loves even when it is rejected. *Agape* love gives and loves because it wants to; it does not demand or expect repayment from the love given - it gives because it loves, it does not love in order to receive.

v. Many people confuse the four loves, and end up extremely hurt as a result. Often a person will tell another, "I love you" meaning one kind of love, but the other person believes he means another kind of love. Often a man has told a woman, "I love you," when really he had a selfish love towards her. Sure, there were strong feelings in the heart - but they were feelings that *wanted* something from the other person.

vi. "It's true you can say to a girl, 'I love you,' but what you really mean is something like this: 'I want something. Not you, but something from you. I don't have time to wait. I want it immediately.' . . . This is the opposite of love, for love wants to give. Love seeks to make the other one happy, and not himself." (Walter Trobisch in *I Loved a Girl*, cited by Boice)

b. **By this we know love, because He laid down His life for us**: Real love isn't merely "felt" as an inward feeling; it is also shown by demonstration - and the ultimate demonstration was the giving of Jesus on the cross.

i. The exact same idea was expressed by Paul in Romans 5:8: *But God demonstrates His own love toward us, in that while we were still sinners, Christ died for us.*

ii. It isn't the death of Jesus in *itself* that is the ultimate demonstration of love; it is the death of Jesus together with *what it does for us* that shows the epitome of love. If I am on a pier, and a man jumps in the water and drowns, and cries out with his last breath, "I'm giving my life for you!" I cannot really comprehend that act as an act of love - it just seems strange. But if that same man jumps in the water to save me from drowning, and gives his own life that I may survive, then I can fully understand how the giving of his life was a great act of love.

iii. In a sermon titled "The Death of Christ for His People," Charles Spurgeon drew three points from this great sentence:

- How great must have been our sins.
- How great must have been His love.
- How safe the believer is in the love of Christ.

c. **By this we know love**: There is a real sense in which we would not **know** what love was all about if not for the work of Jesus on the cross. We have an innate ability to pervert the true meaning of love, and pursue all kinds of things under the guise of looking for love.

i. Nature can teach us many things about God. It can show us His wisdom, His intelligence, and His mighty power. But nature, in and of itself, does not teach us that God is a God of love. We needed the death of God the Son, Jesus Christ, to ultimately demonstrate that.

ii. David Scott Crother died of AIDS in early 1993, but not before he infected his unnamed partner, who pressed charges against Crother. The woman said in an interview: "This is not an assault. It is murder . . . All I wanted is someone to love me, and now I'm going to die for that. I don't think I should have to die for that." We all have that craving for love, but we look for it in the wrong ways and in the wrong places.

d. **And we also**: Since we are sent with the same mandate Jesus was sent with, we must demonstrate our love by laying **down our lives for the brethren**. Jesus' words *As the Father sent Me, I also send you* (John 20:21) seem to be ringing in John's ears.

i. Stott on **laid down** and **lay down**: "It seems to imply not so much the laying *down* as the laying *aside* of something like clothes . . . It is, in fact, used in John 13:4 of Christ taking off his outer garment." [Italics added]

e. **We also ought to lay down our lives for the brethren**: The focus here is on loving **the brethren**. Of course, we are also called to love our enemies and those who hate us (Matthew 5:44), but John calls us to a more basic test - if we can't even love our **brethren**, what kind of Christians are we?

f. **Lay down our lives**: John also reminds us that love, and its demonstration, often involves *sacrifice* - the laying down of our lives for others. *Wishing* to be more loving won't do, because it won't sacrifice where it is necessary.

> i. And if we take the analogy from Jesus' love for us, sometimes the cost of love will make us feel like we are *dying* - but that is what it means to **lay down** your life. "Love means saying 'No' to one's own life so that somebody else may live." (Marshall)

> ii. We often consider ourselves ready to **lay down** our lives in one great, dramatic, heroic gesture; but for most of us, God calls us to lay down our lives piece by piece, little by little in small, but important ways every day.

> iii. Simply put, John is telling us to do the same thing we read of in Philippians 2:3-4: *Let nothing be done through selfish ambition or conceit, but in lowliness of mind let each esteem other better than himself. Let each of you look out not only for his own interests, but also for the interests of others.*

2. (17-18) What it means to love in real life.

**But whoever has this world's goods, and sees his brother in need, and shuts up his heart from him, how does the love of God abide in him? My little children, let us not love in word or in tongue, but in deed and in truth.**

a. **Let us not love in word or in tongue, but in deed and in truth**: John will not allow us to merely *talk* about love; real love is demonstrated in actions (though it is also often evident in our feelings).

b. **And shuts up his heart from him, how does the love of God abide in him?** If you have the capability to meet a brother's needs, and do nothing to meet those needs, then how can you say you love that brother? How **does the love of God abide in** you?

> i. " Here is a test of this love; if we do not divide our bread with the hungry, we certainly would not lay down our life for him. Whatever love we may pretend to mankind, if we are not charitable and benevolent, we give the lie to our profession." (Clarke)

> ii. What is the limit to this kind of love? The only limit is the one that love itself imposes. When giving to a person, meeting his perceived or immediate need, does him harm instead of good - then the loving thing to do is to *not* give him what he asks for, but to give him what he really needs instead.

c. **My little children, let us not love in word or in tongue, but in deed and in truth**: We can substitute talk for love - talking about meeting people's needs instead of actually meeting them.

i. Stott quoting Lewis: "It is easier to be enthusiastic about Humanity with a capital 'H' than it is to love individual men and women, especially those who are uninteresting, exasperating, depraved, or otherwise unattractive. Loving everybody in general may be an excuse for loving nobody in particular."

3. (19-21) The assurance this love brings.

**And by this we know that we are of the truth, and shall assure our hearts before Him. For if our heart condemns us, God is greater than our heart, and knows all things. Beloved, if our heart does not condemn us, we have confidence toward God.**

a. **Assure our hearts**: When we see this love at work in our lives, we can know that we are **of the truth** - and this brings assurance to our hearts before God, that we are standing in Him.

i. Gayle Erwin tells a wonderful story about a man he knew when he was a boy. The man's name was Jake, and he was the meanest, drunkest, man in town. He would come to church from time to time, but that was only to beat up the elders. One Wednesday night, Jake came to church - but not to beat anybody up. Remarkably, Jake gave his life to Jesus. He walked down the aisle of the little church and kneeled down at the altar. The next night there was another meeting at the church, and the pastor asked if anyone wanted to share what God was doing in their lives. Jake stood up, and said: "I have something to say. Last night when I came here, I hated you people." Heads nodded in agreement. "But something happened to me and I don't understand this, but tonight I love you." And even though he only had one tooth, he smiled really big. This is a wonderful assurance that we are born again.

ii. Assurance is essential - who wants to wait until it is too late to know if they are really saved or not?

b. **And shall assure our hearts before Him**: Our assurance is two-fold. First, God *already* knows everything about you and He loves you, He cares for you, He desires you; second, God **knows all things**, and knows who we truly are in Jesus Christ. If we are born again, than the *real* self is the one created in the image of Jesus Christ.

c. **For if our heart condemns us, God is greater than our heart, and knows all things**: But what if we have been walking in love, yet our heart still condemns us before God? John assures us that **God is greater than our heart**, and so reminds us that we cannot base our relationship with Him purely on how we *feel* in His presence.

i. Condemnation can well up inside us that has nothing to do with our standing before God. It may be the work of the enemy of our souls (who, according to Revelation 12:10 accuses the brethren), or the work of an over-active conscience. At those times, we trust in what God's Word says about our standing, not how we feel about it.

ii. "Sometimes our heart condemns us, but, in doing so, it gives a wrong verdict, and then we have the satisfaction of being able to take the case into a higher court, for 'God is greater than our heart, and knoweth all things.' " (Spurgeon)

d. **Beloved, if our heart does not condemn us, we have confidence toward God**: Yet, when we are in fellowship with God, and **our heart does not condemn us**, we know that we can have confidence toward God and our standing with Him.

i. If someone is in true fellowship with God - not deceiving oneself, as mentioned in 1 John 1:6 - then the assurance that comes to his heart while fellowshipping with God is a precious thing. It is what Paul spoke about in Romans 8:16 - *The Spirit Himself bears witness with our spirit that we are children of God.*

e. **We have confidence toward God**: How precious is the **confidence** we can have in Jesus Christ! There is such a thing as a false confidence, a confidence in self or in illusions; but there is also a glorious **confidence** we can have in Jesus.

i. "The word rendered *confidence* stood in ancient Greece for the most valued right of a citizen of a free state, the right to 'speak his mind' . . . unhampered by fear or shame." (Barker citing Dodd)

4. (22) Fellowship in God's love means the assurance of answered prayer.

**And whatever we ask we receive from Him, because we keep His commandments and do those things that are pleasing in His sight.**

a. **Whatever we ask**: The person who walks in the kind of obedience and love John speaks of will also experience answered prayer. This is not because their love and obedience has *earned* them what they ask, but their love and obedience comes from fellowship - the key to answered prayer.

i. John seems to be quoting Jesus' idea from John 15:7 - *If you abide in Me, and My words abide in you, you will ask what you desire, and it shall be done for you.*

b. **Because we keep His commandments**: Keeping God's commandments is important to answered prayer. But we should make a distinction between the prayer of the man who is saved, and the cry of the heart seeking mercy from God in Jesus. For the sinner who comes to Jesus in prayer, seeking mercy, the only requirement is sincerity of heart. God does not demand our obedience *before* He saves us.

> i. The key to prayer is being in such close fellowship with God that we ask for the things that are on *His* heart; we take up His agenda with our requests and intercession.

> ii. The spirit of true prayer is *Thy will be done*, not *My will be done* - we turn to prayer to call into action what God desires; even knowing that some of the things God desires will directly and personally benefit us.

c. **And do those things that are pleasing in His sight**: The person who is in fellowship with God will want to **do those things that are pleasing in His sight**. We should have hearts that just want to please the Lord in everything that we do.

> i. It is sobering to look at our lives and see how much we do to please ourselves and how much we do to please the Lord. We shouldn't think that the two are opposites; God is glorified when we enjoy His goodness and His good things. Yet, the godly life will have special focus on just pleasing God, even if it doesn't particularly please us at the moment.

5. (23-24) The commandment of Jesus.

**And this is His commandment: that we should believe on the name of His Son Jesus Christ and love one another, as He gave us commandment. Now he who keeps His commandments abides in Him, and He in him. And by this we know that He abides in us, by the Spirit whom He has given us.**

a. **And this is His commandment**: The idea of keeping *His commandments* in the previous verse led John to speak specifically about what **His commandment** is. Simply, that **we should believe on the name of His Son Jesus Christ and love one another**.

> i. Here, John does not refer to these two aspects of obedience as two commandments, but as one **commandment**. Grammatically, he may not be officially correct, but spiritually, he is right on. These two are one. When Jesus spoke of the greatest commandment: *You shall love the* LORD *your God with all your heart, with all your soul, and with all your mind,* He added another saying: *And the second is like it: "You shall love your neighbor as yourself"* (Matthew 22:37-39). There are two commandments, but they are clearly *like* one another.

b. **We should believe on the name of His Son**: Again, John seems to have quoted Jesus' idea from John 6:29: *This is the work of God, that you believe in Him whom He sent.* The first commandment and the greatest work we can do, is to believe on Jesus.

i. This is not simply believing that Jesus is, or even believing that He did certain things such as die on a cross. To **believe on the name of** Jesus means to put your belief **on** Jesus in the sense of trusting in Him, relying on Him, and clinging to Jesus. It isn't about intellectual knowledge or understanding, it is about *trust*.

c. **And love one another**: The second commandment is also a quoting of Jesus' idea from John 15:12: *This is My commandment, that you love one another as I have loved you.* The love of the brethren is not an option for some Christians; it is a commandment for all.

d. **Abides in Him**: Those who abide in Jesus *know* they are abiding in Jesus, because of the presence and assurance of the Holy Spirit. John again is giving the same idea as Romans 8:16 (*The Spirit Himself bears witness with our spirit that we are children of God*).

i. Romans 8:9 tells us that anyone who belongs to Jesus has the Spirit in him; that indwelling Holy Spirit gives us assurance. You can't be abiding in Jesus and not know it, though you may be attacked with doubt from time to time.

ii. The one who does *not* keep God's commandments does not have the ground of confidence that he abides in Jesus. As well, he does not truly have the assurance of the Holy Spirit's presence in his life.

iii. To know if you really have this assurance can take spiritual discernment, and that is what John deals with in the very next verse. But God has already given us another basis for assurance: seeing if we love one another (1 John 3:19).

# *1 John 4 - Abiding in God and His Love*

A. Protection against the spirit of truth and the spirit of error.

1. (1) The fact of false prophets and the need to test the spirits.

**Beloved, do not believe every spirit, but test the spirits, whether they are of God; because many false prophets have gone out into the world.**

a. **Do not believe every spirit**: John warned against believing **every spirit**; that is, we are never to assume every spiritual experience or every demonstration of spiritual power is from God. We must test spiritual experiences and spiritual phenomenon to see if they are in fact from God.

i. Many, when first encountering the *reality* of the spiritual world, are too impressed and amazed to ask **whether they are of God**. This leads to easy deception.

b. **But test the spirits**: This is important because **many false prophets have gone out into the world**. Even though the early church had a strong life and a large measure of purity, John still knew the danger false prophets and their message was real in the early church.

c. **Test the spirits, whether they are of God**: This is the responsibility of every Christian, but especially of congregational leadership. According to 1 Corinthians 14:29 (*let the others judge*) and 1 Thessalonians 5:21 (*Test all things; hold fast what is good*), testing the spirits is the work of the body of Christ. This job is to be done using the gifts of discernment God has given to Christians in general, especially the leadership of a congregation.

i. All prophecy is to be judged by Scriptural standards. It is never to be received just because it is dramatic or given by a certain person. We trust in the principle that God will never contradict Himself, and we *know* what He has already said in His Word.

ii. 2 Peter 1:20-21 tells us true prophecy is never *of any private interpretation*. This means that there will be agreement and confirmation from the body of Christ, though perhaps (or probably) not *everyone* will agree or confirm.

2. (2-3) How to know when a false prophet speaks.

**By this you know the Spirit of God: Every spirit that confesses that Jesus Christ has come in the flesh is of God, and every spirit that does not confess that Jesus Christ has come in the flesh is not of God. And this is the *spirit* of the Antichrist, which you have heard was coming, and is now already in the world.**

a. **Every spirit that confesses that Jesus Christ has come in the flesh is of God**: True prophecy, and true teaching, will present a true Jesus. In John's day, the issue was about if Jesus had *truly* come in a *real* body of flesh and blood. Many Gnostic-influenced teachers said that Jesus, being God, could not have actually become a flesh and blood human being, because God could have no partnership with "impure" material stuff.

i. "This statement would be directed against some form of Docetism, the view that Christ was a spirit who only seemed to be a true man." (Boice)

ii. Today, some groups deny that Jesus is really God (such as the Jehovah's Witnesses, Mormons, and Muslims). But way back in John's day, in this time closest to the actual life and ministry of Jesus on this earth, people didn't have a hard time believing Jesus was God. They had a hard time believing that he was a *real* man. This false teaching said Jesus was truly God (which is correct), but really a "make-believe" man.

iii. Today, we are passionate about saying, "Jesus is God," and we should be. But it is no less important to say, "Jesus is a man," because both the deity and humanity of Jesus are essential to our salvation.

b. **Every spirit that confesses that Jesus Christ has come in the flesh is of God**: Some think that this is the *only* test of false doctrine. This is not the only test, but it was the significant issue challenging the church in John's immediate time. Today a person might **confess that Jesus Christ has come in the flesh** yet deny that He is God as the Bible teaches He is God. They also are giving false doctrine because they are not presenting a *true Jesus*.

i. The principle of presenting a *true Jesus* is essential to the testing of spirits. No one who presents a false Jesus, or one untrue to the Scriptures, can be regarded as a true prophet.

ii. Today, there is a lot of curiosity about the "true Jesus." Many modern academics say they want to discover the "true Jesus" and when they say this they often mean, "The true Jesus is not the Jesus of the Bible. The Biblical Jesus is make-believe. We need to discover the *true* Jesus behind the myths of the Bible."

iii. Not only is this position *ignorant* (ignoring the confirmed historical validity of the New Testament) it is also *arrogant*. Once any academic throws out the historical evidence of the New Testament and other reliable ancient writings, they can only base their understanding of Jesus on their *own personal opinion*. These academics present their *baseless opinions* as if they were *scholarly facts*.

c. **This is the spirit of the Antichrist**: To deny the true Jesus is the basis of the **spirit of the Antichrist**, which John has already mentioned in 1 John 2:18-23. It is the spirit which both *opposes* the true Jesus and offers a *substitute* Jesus.

i. The devil doesn't care at all if you know Jesus or love Jesus or pray to Jesus — as long as it is a *false* Jesus, a *make-believe* Jesus, a Jesus who is not there, and who therefore *cannot save*.

d. **Is now already in the world**: Though it will have its ultimate consummation in an end-times political and economic ruler, the essence of this antichrist **spirit** is present with us today. It is found everywhere a false Jesus is promoted in place of the true Jesus of the Bible.

3. (4) The protection of the child of God.

**You are of God, little children, and have overcome them, because He who is in you is greater than he who is in the world.**

a. **You are of God, little children, and have overcome them**: The child of God need not fear the *spirit of Antichrist*, even though they should be warned of it, because they have the indwelling Spirit of God (1 John 3:24). That indwelling Spirit is greater than **he who is in the world** - Satan and all of his allies.

b. **He who is in you is greater than he who is in the world**: The believer has a resource for victory, the vital presence of the indwelling Jesus, which makes victory always possible — *if* we will rely on **He who is in you** instead of relying on ourselves.

i. This understanding gives great confidence and spiritual power. For those walking in this truth, victory is assured - they **have overcome them**. It is a positive statement, not a wishful hope.

c. **He who is in you is greater than he who is in the world**: This means the Christian has no place for fear. We have many spiritual enemies, but not *one* of them is greater than Jesus who lives in us.

i. Earlier in the letter, John brought up the idea of the world and its threat to the Christian life (1 John 2:15-17). He presented the **world** not as the global earth or the mass of humanity, which God Himself loves (John 3:16). Instead it is the community of sinful humanity that is united in rebellion against God. Here, John suggests that there are forces of spiritual darkness that guide and influence **the world**.

4. (5-6) The contrast between those in the world and those who are of God.

**They are of the world. Therefore they speak *as* of the world, and the world hears them. We are of God. He who knows God hears us; he who is not of God does not hear us. By this we know the spirit of truth and the spirit of error.**

a. **They are of the world**: Those who are **of the world** are evident because they **speak as of the world**; the influence of the world in evident in their speech. As Jesus said, *out of the abundance of the heart the mouth speaks* (Matthew 12:34).

b. **And the world hears them**: Those who are **of the world** are also evident because the **world hears them**. They face none of the rejection the child of God will face from the world (1 John 3:1), because they are friends with the world.

i. **The world hears them**: The Christian always wants to speak to the world, and to bring the gospel of Jesus Christ to the world. It is exciting when the world will listen to the gospel, but we must take care that they are not hearing us because we **speak as of the world**. Just because the world is hearing the message doesn't prove that the message is God's message.

c. **He who knows God hears us**: Those who are **of God** enjoy fellowship with other believers; they speak the common language of fellowship with God and with each other, because one flows from the other (1 John 1:3).

i. This language of fellowship transcends language, culture, class, race, or any other barrier. It is a true gift from God.

ii. In its official doctrines, the Roman Catholic Church has claimed to be the "**us**" in **He who knows God hears us; he who is not of God does not hear us**. But John can only be talking about the apostles and their authoritative revelation in the Bible when he says **us**. When we know God, and are of God, we hear what the Bible says.

iii. "If this were a mere individual talking, the claim would be presumptuous. But it is not. This is one of the apostles citing the collective testimony of all the apostles and making that testimony the measure of truth and sound doctrine." (Boice)

d. **He who is not of God does not hear us**: Understanding just who hears what God has taught us through the apostles, as recorded in the New Testament, helps us to know the **spirit of truth and the spirit of error**. If someone hears what God has said in the Bible, we know he has the **spirit of truth**. If he does not hear it, he has the **spirit of error**.

i. John makes it clear that **error** has a *spiritual* dynamic to it; it isn't just about being educated or smart. Some very educated, very smart people can still be influence mightily by the **spirit of error**. Since error has a spiritual dynamic to it, keeping in the **spirit of truth** is a spiritual issue.

ii. We keep in the **spirit of truth** by clinging to Jesus, the One who said *I am the truth* (John 14:6).

B. Love perfected among us.

1. (7-8) The call to love.

**Beloved, let us love one another, for love is of God; and everyone who loves is born of God and knows God. He who does not love does not know God, for God is love.**

a. **Beloved, let us love**: The ancient Greek sentence begins in a striking way - *agapetoi agapomen*, "those who are loved, let us love." We are not commanded to **love one another** to earn or become worthy of God's love. We **love one another** because we are loved by God, and have received that love, and live in light of it.

b. **Let us love one another, for love is of God**: John's emphasis on love among the people of God (shown in passages like 1 John 2:9-11 and 3:10-18) is powerful. Here, he shows *why* it is so important. If **love is of God**, then those who claim to be **born of God**, and claim to **know God**, must be able to **love one another** in the body of Christ.

i. Again, John insists that there is something that is given to the believer when they are **born of God**; a love is imparted to their life that they did not have before. Christians are not "*just* forgiven" - they are born anew by God's Spirit.

c. **And knows God**: There are several different words in the ancient Greek language translated "know" into English. This specific word for **knows** (*ginosko*) is the word for a knowledge by *experience*. John is saying when we really experience God it will show by our love for **one another**.

i. Of course, this love is not perfected in the life of a Christian on this side of eternity. Though it may not be perfected, it must be present — and it should be growing. You can't truly grow in your *experience* of God without also growing love for **one another**. John can boldly say, **He who does not love does not know God**. If there isn't real love for God's people in your life, then your claim to know God and experience God isn't true.

d. **Love is of God**: The love John speaks of comes from the ancient Greek word *agape*; it is the concept of a self-giving love that gives without demanding or expecting re-payment - it is the God-kind of love.

i. Since this is God's kind of love, it comes into our life through our relationship with Him. If we want to **love one another** more, we need to draw closer to God.

ii. Every human relationship is like a triangle. The two people in the relationship are at the base of the triangle, and God is at the top. As the two people draw closer to the top of the triangle, closer to God, they will also draw closer to one another. Weak relationships are made strong when both people draw close to the Lord!

e. **Everyone who loves is born of God . . . He who does not love does not know God**: This does not mean that every display of love in the world can only come from a Christian. Those who are not Christians still can display acts of love.

i. "It is because men are created in the image of God, an image that has been defaced but not destroyed by the Fall, that they still have the capacity to love . . . Human love, however noble and however highly motivated, falls short if it refuses to include the Father and Son as the supreme objects of its affection." (Marshall)

f. **For God is love**: This is a glorious truth. Love describes the character and heart of God. He is so rich in love and compassion, that it can be used to describe His very being.

i. When we say **God is love**, we are not saying *everything* about God. Love is an essential aspect of His character, and colors every aspect of His nature. But it does not eliminate His holiness, His righteousness, or His perfect justice. Instead, we know the holiness of God is loving, and the righteousness of God is loving, and the justice of God is loving. Everything God does, in one way or another, expresses His love.

ii. "He hates nothing he has made. He cannot *hate*, because he is *love*. He causes the sun to rise on the evil and the good, and sends his rain on the just and the unjust. He has made no human being for perdition, nor ever rendered it impossible, by any necessitating decree, for a fallen soul to find mercy. He has given the fullest proof of his love to the whole human race by the incarnation of his Son, who tasted death for every man. How can a *decree* of absolute, unconditional *reprobation*, of the greater part or any part of the human race, stand in the presence of such a text as this?" (Clarke)

iii. "Never let it be thought that any sinner is beyond the reach of divine mercy so long as he is in the land of the living. I stand here to preach illimitable love, unbounded grace, to the vilest of the vile, to those who have nothing in them that can deserve consideration from God, men who ought to be swept into the bottomless pit at once if justice meted out to them their deserts." (Spurgeon)

iv. Great problems come when we try to say *love is God*. This is because love does not define *everything* in the character of God, and because when most people use the term *love*, they are not thinking of true love, the God-kind of love. Instead, they are thinking of a squishy, namby-pamby, have-a-nice-day kind of love that values being "nice" more than wanting what is really best for the other person.

v. The Bible also tells us that God is *spirit* (John 4:24), God is *light* (1 John 1:5), and that God is *a consuming fire* (Hebrews 12:29).

g. **God is love**: There are few people who really know and really believe that **God is love**. For whatever reason, they won't receive His love and let it transform their lives. It transforms our life to know the love of God in this way.

i. "There is love in many places, like wandering beams of light; but as for the sun, it is in one part of the heavens, and we look at it, and we say, 'Herein is light.' . . . He did not look at the Church of God, and say of all the myriads who counted not their lives dear unto them, 'Herein is love,' for their love was only the reflected brightness of the great sun of love." (Spurgeon)

2. (9-11) The meaning of love and its application.

**In this the love of God was manifested toward us, that God has sent His only begotten Son into the world, that we might live through Him. In this is love, not that we loved God, but that He loved us and sent His Son *to be* the propitiation for our sins. Beloved, if God so loved us, we also ought to love one another.**

a. **In this the love of God was manifested toward us, that God sent His only begotten Son**: This shows us what love is and what it means. Love is not only defined by the sacrifice of Jesus (as stated in 1 John 3:16); it is also defined by the giving of the Father. It was a sacrifice for the Father to send the Second Person of the Trinity, and a sacrifice to pour out the judgment we deserved upon God the Son.

i. We need to appreciate this fully, and receive the Fatherly love God has to give us. Some of us, for whatever reason, have come to think of God the Father as aloof and mean, perhaps the so-called "angry God" of the Old Testament. In this wrong thinking, many imagine they prefer the nice and loving Jesus instead. But the Father loves us too; and the love Jesus showed in His ministry was the same love God the Father has towards us. We can receive the healing power in our Father's love.

b. **That God has sent His only begotten Son into the world**: John is careful to call Jesus the **only begotten Son**. This special term means Jesus has a Sonship that is unique (**only**) and **begotten** indicates that Jesus and the Father are of the same substance, the same essential Being.

i. We use the term *create* to describe something that may come from someone, but isn't of the same essential nature or being. A man can *create* a statue that looks just like him, but it will never be human. However, we use the term *beget* to describe something that is *exactly* the same as us in essential nature and being. We are *adopted* sons and daughters of God, but we are not of the same essential nature and being as God — we are human beings. But Jesus is the **only begotten Son**, meaning His Sonship is different than ours; He was and is of the same essential nature and being as God the Father. We are human beings; He is a "God-being" — who added humanity to His deity.

c. **That we might live through Him**: The love of the Father was not only in the sending of the Son, but also in what that sending accomplishes for us. It brings life to all who trust in Jesus and His work on their behalf, because He is **the propitiation for our sins**.

i. **Propitiation** has the idea of a sacrifice that turns away the wrath of God. God rightly regarded us, apart from Him, as worthy targets of His judgment. We were rebels and enemies of Him, even if we didn't know it. But on the cross, Jesus took the punishment our sin deserved — His sacrifice turned away the judgment we would have received. We easily think how this shows the love of Jesus, but John wants us to understand it also shows the love of God the Father: **He loved us and sent His Son to be the propitiation for our sins**.

ii. **That we might live through Him**: The greatness of God's love is shown not only in saving us from the judgment we deserved, but also in wanting us to **live through Him**. Do we **live through Him**? This is a great way to define the Christian life, to **live through Him**.

d. **God has sent His only begotten Son**: This shows the love of God, because love gives its best. There was nothing better God the Father could give to lost humanity than the gift of the Son of God Himself. As Paul describes it in 2 Corinthians 9:15, Jesus was the Father's *indescribable gift*.

i. "If there was to be reconciliation between God and man, man ought to have sent to God; the offender ought to be the first to apply for forgiveness; the weaker should apply to the greater for help; the poor man should ask of him who distributes alms; but 'Herein is love' that God 'sent.' He was first to send an embassy of peace." (Spurgeon)

e. **He loved us and sent His Son to be the propitiation for our sins**: This shows the love of God. It might have shown enough love that the Father sent the Son, and not some lower-grade angel; but He sent the Son, not on a fact-finding mission or merely a mission of compassion – He sent the Son to *die* for our sins.

> i. "If God had merely sent Jesus to teach us about Himself, that would have been wonderful enough. It would have been far more than we deserved. If God had sent Jesus simply to be our example, that would have been good too and would have had some value . . . But the wonderful thing is that God did not stop with these but rather sent His Son, not merely to teach or to be our example, but to die the death of a felon, that He might save us from sin." (Boice)

f. **For our sins**: This shows the love of God. God gave His Son to die, and to die for *sinners*. We can think of someone paying a great price to save someone deserving, someone good, someone noble, someone who had done much for them. But God did all this for rebels, for sinners, for those who had turned their backs on Him.

> i. "But who among us would think of giving up his son to die for his enemy, for one who never did him a service, but treated him ungratefully, repulsed a thousand overtures of tenderness, and went on perversely hardening his neck? No man could do it." (Spurgeon)

g. **In this is love**: Real love, *agape* love, is not defined by our love for God, but by His love for us. His love for us initiates our relationship of love with Him, our love only responds to His love for us. We can't love God the way we should unless we are receiving and living in His love.

> i. Our love for God doesn't really say anything great about us. It is only the common sense response to knowing and receiving the love of God.

h. **If God so loved us**: Having received this love from God, we are directed to **love one another**. This pattern of receiving from God, then giving to others was familiar to John (John 13:14).

> i. When Jesus washed the feet of the disciples, and showed such great love and servanthood to them, we might have expected Him to conclude by gesturing to His own feet and asking who among them was going to do to Him what He had just done for them. Instead, Jesus said: *If I then, your Lord and Teacher, have washed your feet, you also ought to wash one another's feet* (John 13:14). The proper way to love God in response to His love for us is to go out and **love one another**.

ii. This love will lead to practical action. "Has anybody offended you? Seek reconciliation. 'Oh, but I am the offended party.' So was God, and he went straight away and sought reconciliation. Brother, do the same. 'Oh, but I have been insulted.' Just so: so was God: all the wrong was towards him, yet he sent. 'Oh, but the party is so unworthy.' So are you; but 'God loved you and sent his Son.' Go write according to that copy." (Spurgeon)

iii. If we do not **love one another**, how can we say that we have received the love of God and have been born of Him? Love is the proof we are taught to look for. If you had a pipe that was clogged – water kept going into it, but never came out, that pipe would be useless. You would replace it. Just so, God puts His love into our lives that it might flow out. We want the Lord to clear us and fill us so that His love can flow through us.

C. The nature of a love relationship with God.

1. (12) Seeing God through the evidence of love.

**No one has seen God at any time. If we love one another, God abides in us, and His love has been perfected in us.**

a. **No one has seen God at any time**: John relates a basic principle about God the Father – that no one, **no one**, **has seen God at any time**. Anyone claiming to have seen God the Father is speaking – at best – from their own imagination, because as John plainly states, **no one has seen God at any time.**

i. In speaking of God the Father, Paul wrote in 1 Timothy 1:17: *Now to the King eternal, immortal, invisible.* Jesus declared of God the Father, *God is Spirit*, (John 4:24) meaning that God the Father has no tangible body which may be seen.

ii. Knowing God the Father is invisible should make us more humble in our relationship with Him. God the Father is not completely knowable by us; we can't completely figure out God, or know all His secrets. He is beyond us.

iii. Of course, no one has seen God the Holy Spirit at any time either, though He has represented Himself in various ways. And just as certainly, God the Son, Jesus Christ, *has* been seen – John himself testified to this in 1 John 1:1-3. But of God the Father, it can truly be said, **no one has seen God at any time.**

iv. "The Old Testament theophanies, including the apparently contradictory statement in Exodus 24:10, did not involve the full revelation of God as He is in Himself but only a suggestion of what He is in form that a human being could understand." (Boice)

b. **If we love one another, God abides in us**: This is the greatest evidence of God's presence and work among us - **love**. Since no one **has seen God at any time**, this provides evidence for the presence of God.

> i. Some people think the greatest evidence of God's presence or work is *power*. Some people think the greatest evidence of God's presence or work is *popularity*. Some people think the greatest evidence of God's presence or work is *passionate feelings*. But the greatest evidence of God's presence and work is **love**. Where God is present and working, there will be love.
>
> ii. Sometimes Jesus seemed weak and lacking in power, but He was always full of love. Sometimes Jesus wasn't popular at all, but He was always full of love. Sometimes Jesus didn't inspire passionate feelings in people at all, but He was always full of love. Love was the constant, greatest evidence of the presence and work of God in Jesus Christ.

c. **His love has been perfected in us**: **Perfected** uses the Greek word *teleioo*, which doesn't mean "perfect" as much as "mature" and "complete." If we **love one another**, then the love of God is "mature" and "complete" in us.

> i. John comes back to the familiar idea: if we really walk in God's love towards us, it will be evident in our love for one another.
>
> ii. The mature Christian will be marked by love. Again, the true measure of maturity is not the image of power, or popularity, or passionate feelings – but the abiding presence of God's love in our lives, given out to others.

2. (13-15) Assurance of the work of the Triune God in us.

**By this we know that we abide in Him, and He in us, because He has given us of His Spirit. And we have seen and testify that the Father has sent the Son *as* Savior of the world. Whoever confesses that Jesus is the Son of God, God abides in him, and he in God.**

a. **We know we abide in Him**: By beginning with the words **by this**, John connected the thought of this verse directly to the previous verse. We can *know by experience* that we live in God, if *His love has been perfected in us*. And we know that *His love has been perfected in us* if we *love one another*.

> i. Plainly, Christians can say, **"We know."** We don't have to merely "hope" we are saved, and "hope" we will make it to heaven, thus having no assurance of salvation before we pass from this world to the next. We can **know**, and we can **know** now, on *this* side of eternity.

b. **We abide in Him, and He in us**: Our abiding in Jesus is not a one-sided affair, with us struggling to abide in Him, and Jesus trying to escape us. Just as true as it is that we should **abide in Him**, it is true that He does abide **in us**.

> i. Jesus said in John 15:4, *Abide in Me, and I in you.* And in John 15:7, He said, *If you abide in Me, and My words abide in you.* One of the ways Jesus abides in us – lives in us – is through His word.

c. **He has given us of His Spirit**: John brings up the work of the Holy Spirit in us at this point for two important connections. First, it is the Spirit of God in us that is the abiding presence of Jesus – the presence of His Spirit is *how* He abides in us. Secondly, it is the testimony of the Holy Spirit within us that makes it possible for us to **know that we abide in Him**. As Paul puts it in Roman 8:16: *The Spirit Himself bears witness with our spirit that we are children of God.* The Holy Spirit gives us this assurance.

d. **We have seen and testify**: The "**we**" who give testimony in this verse are those who saw Jesus originally, the eyewitnesses to His presence. They *knew* **the Father sent the Son as Savior of the world**.

e. **We have seen and testify**: Speaking as one who has the Spirit of God (**He has given us of His Spirit**), John declares three essential truths about who God is and how He saves us.

> (1) **That the Father has sent the Son.**

> (2) That He (Jesus) was sent **as Savior of the world**.

> (3) Knowing and understanding Jesus is the foundation for abiding in Him (**Whoever confesses that Jesus is the Son of God, God abides in him, and he in God**).

f. **Whoever confesses that Jesus is the Son of God, God abides in him, and he in God**: It isn't enough to *know* the facts about who Jesus is; we must *confess* the truth. The idea behind the word *confess* is "to be in agreement with." We must agree with God about who Jesus is, and we find out what God says about Jesus through the Word of God. You may *know* something without being in *agreement* with it; God demands our true *agreement*.

> i. Though John has been writing much about love, he does not ignore the issue of *truth*. John does not think it is "enough" if a person has some kind of love in his life if he does not **confess that Jesus is the Son of God**. It isn't a matter of deciding between love or truth; we must have both.

> ii. "To acknowledge that Jesus is the Son of God is not simply to make a statement about his metaphysical status but to express obedient trust in the One who possesses such a status." (Marshall)

> iii. "To believe in Christ and to love the brethren are not conditions by which we may dwell in God but rather are evidences of the fact that

God has already taken possession of our lives to make this possible." (Boice)

3. (16) The Christian's response to God and His love.

**And we have known and believed the love that God has for us. God is love, and he who abides in love abides in God, and God in him.**

a. **And we have known and believed the love God has for us**: This is the Christian's proper response to who God is, and how He loves us. We are called to take the love and grace God gives, to know it by experience and to believe it. This is what fellowship with God is all about.

i. People respond to the love of God differently.

- Some respond with a sense of self-superiority ("I'm so great, even God loves me!").

- Some respond with doubt ("Can God really love even me?").

- Some respond with wickedness ("God loves me, so I can do what I want").

- God wants us to respond by *knowing* (by experience) and *believing* **the love God has for us**.

ii. The Christian must *know* and *believe* **the love God has for us**. We should consider what would it take to make us *stop* believing God loves us. Paul knew that *nothing* could separate him from the love of God that was in Jesus Christ (Romans 8:35-39), and each Christian should have the same confidence.

iii. "To feel God's love is very precious, but to believe it when you do not feel it, is the noblest." (Spurgeon)

b. **He who abides in love abides in God, and God in him**: The Christian who has this kind of relationship with God will be virtually "immersed" in God's love; it becomes his environment, his place of abiding.

4. (17-18) The perfecting of love, both now and in eternity.

**Love has been perfected among us in this: that we may have boldness in the day of judgment; because as He is, so are we in this world. There is no fear in love; but perfect love casts out fear, because fear involves torment. But he who fears has not been made perfect in love.**

a. **Love has been perfected**: For **perfected**, John doesn't just use the Greek word *teleioo* (which has the idea of "maturity" and "completeness"); he writes *teleioo teleioo* – speaking of love that is "perfectly perfected" or "completely complete."

b. **In the day of judgment**: This is *when* the completeness of love's work in us will be demonstrated. As much as we can know the completeness of God's love now, we will know it all the more **in the day of judgment**.

- You may know you are a sinner now; you will really *know* it **in the day of judgment**.

- You may know now you are not a better person than those who are going to hell; you will really *know* it **in the day of judgment**.

- You may know the reality of hell now; you will really *know* it **in the day of judgment**.

- You may know the greatness of Jesus' salvation now; you will really *know* it **in the day of judgment**.

c. **That we may have boldness in the day of judgment**: This shows the greatness of God's work in us. We might be satisfied to merely *survive* the **day of judgment**, but God wants to so fill our lives with His love and His truth that we have **boldness in the day of judgment**.

i. The Bible says that one day, all of humanity will gather before God's *Great White Throne* and face judgment. This day is coming! "The day of judgment is as fixed in God's eternal timetable as any other day in world history." (Boice)

ii. Some think they will go there and judge *God* ("When I seen God, there's a few questions I have for Him!"), but that is nonsense. The only way to have **boldness in the day of judgment** is to receive, and walk in, the transforming love of God *today*.

d. **Boldness in the day of judgment**: How can anyone have such **boldness**? We can imagine Jesus being bold before the throne of God, but us? Yet, if *we abide in Him, and He in us* (1 John 4:13), then our identity is bound up in Jesus: **as He is, so are we in the world**.

i. How **is** Jesus now? He is glorified, justified, forever righteous and bold, sitting at the right hand of God the Father. Spiritually, we can have that same standing *now*, while we are **in the world**, because **as He is, so are we in the world**.

ii. Certainly, this glory is in us now just in "seed" form; it has not yet fully developed into what it will be. But it is there, and its presence is demonstrated by our love for one another and our agreement with God's truth – and that all serves to give us **boldness**.

e. **There is no fear in love**: The completeness of love means we do not cower in fear before God, dreading His judgment, either now or **in the**

**day of judgment**. We know all the judgment we ever deserved – past, present, and future – was poured out on Jesus Christ on the cross.

i. What about the many passages of Scripture, Old and New Testament (such as Ecclesiastes 12:13 and 1 Peter 2:17), which tell us we should *fear God*? The **fear** John writes of here is not the appropriate reverence we should all have of God, but the kind of fear which **involves torment** - that agonizing kind of fear which robs our soul of all joy and confidence before God. It is the **fear** that is the opposite of **boldness in the day of judgment.**

f. **But he who fears has not been made perfect in love**: If our relationship with God is marked by this tormenting fear, it shows that we have not been **made perfect** - that is, complete, and mature - in His love.

*Charles Spurgeon was a man who preached the whole counsel of God's Word, and was careful to not excessively repeat himself in any one area. Yet, he preached five remarkable sermons on these eight words alone.*

5. (19) The reason for our love to Jesus.

**We love Him because He first loved us.**

a. *We* **love Him**: In this great statement, John begins by declaring the heart of every true follower of Jesus Christ. Simply and boldly put, **we love Him**.

i. This is a fact for *every* true follower of Jesus. "There is no exception to this rule; if a man loves not God, neither is he born of God. Show me a fire without heat, then show me regeneration that does not produce love to God." (Spurgeon)

ii. It is something that every Christian should be unafraid to proclaim: "I love Him; I love Jesus." Can you say that? Are you embarrassed to say it? Can you say, "I love Jesus"?

iii. "I cannot imagine a true man saying, 'I love Christ, but I do not want others to know that I love him, lest they should laugh at me.' That is a reason to be laughed at, or rather, to be wept over. Afraid of being laughed at? Oh sir, this is indeed a cowardly fear!" (Spurgeon)

iv. "Look through all the pages of history, and put to the noblest men and women, who seem to still live, this question, 'Who loves Christ?' and, at once, up from dark dungeons and cruel racks there rises the confessors' cry, 'We love him;' and from the fiery stake, where they clapped their hands as they were being burned to death, the same answer comes, 'We love him.' If you could walk through the miles of catacombs at Rome, and if the holy dead, whose dust lies there, could suddenly wake up, they would all shout, 'We love him.' The best and the bravest of men, the noblest and purest of women, have all been in this glorious company; so, surely, you are not ashamed to come forward and say, 'Put my name down among them.' " (Spurgeon)

v. "Be out-and-out for him; unfurl your colours, never hide them, but nail them to the mast, and say to all who ridicule the saints, 'If you have any ill words for the followers of Christ, pour them out upon me. . . . but know this – ye shall hear it whether you like it or not, - "I love Christ." ' " (Spurgeon)

b. **He first loved us**: This verse not only declares our love for Jesus, it also tells us *when* He loved us. Some people imagine that Jesus loved us because He knew we would love Him and come to faith in Him. But He loved us before that, and even before the worlds were created, when our only existence was in the mind and heart of God, Jesus loved us.

i. He loved us when we were still sinners: "Every man that ever was saved had to come to God not as a lover of God, but as a sinner, and then believe in God's love to him as a sinner." (Spurgeon)

ii. "Jesus loved you when you lived carelessly, when you neglected his Word, when the knee was unbent in prayer. Ah! He loved some of you when you were in the dancing saloon, when you were in the playhouse, ay, even when you were in the brothel. He loved you when you were at hell's gate, and drank damnation at every draught. He loved you when you could not have been worse or further from him than you were. Marvellous, O Christ, is thy strange love!" (Spurgeon)

c. **We love Him because He first loved us**: This verse tells us *where* our love for Jesus comes from. It comes from *Him*. Our love for God is always in *response* to His love for us; He initiates, and we respond. We never have to draw God to us; instead, He draws us to Himself.

i. "1. We love him because we find he has loved us. 2. We love him from a sense of obligation and gratitude. 3. We love him from the influence of his own love; from his love shed abroad in our hearts our love to him proceeds. It is the seed whence our love springs." (Clarke)

ii. "His is the fountain love, ours but the stream: his love the inducement, the pattern, and the effective cause of ours. He that is first in love, loves freely; the other therefore loves under obligation." (Poole)

iii. "I have sometimes noticed that, in addressing Sunday-school children, it is not uncommon to tell them that the way to be saved is to love Jesus, which is not true. The way to be saved for man, woman, or child is to trust Jesus for the pardon of sin, and then, trusting Jesus, love comes as a fruit. Love is by no means the root. Faith alone occupies that place." (Spurgeon)

d. **We love Him** *because* **He first loved us**: This verse tells us *why* we love Jesus, and *how* we can love Him more.

    i. "Love believed is the mother of love returned." (Spurgeon)

    ii. "Yet we must not try to make ourselves love our Lord, but look to Christ's love first, for his love to us will beget in us love to him. I know that some of you are greatly distressed because you cannot love Christ as much as you would like to do, and you keep on fretting because it is so. Now, just forget your own love to him, and think of his great love to you; and then, immediately, your love will come to something more like that which you would desire it to be." (Spurgeon)

    iii. "Now remember, we never make ourselves love Christ more by flogging ourselves for not loving him more. We come to love those better whom we love by knowing them better . . . If you want to love Christ more, think more of him, think more of what you have received from him." (Spurgeon)

e. **He first loved us**: This means that it is true that He loves us now. Do you believe it? "Oh, if you do really believe that he has loved you so, sit down, and turn the subject over in your mind, and say to yourself, 'Jesus loves me; Jesus chose me; Jesus redeemed me; Jesus called me; Jesus has pardoned me; Jesus has taken me into union with himself.' " (Spurgeon)

6. (20-21) The commandment to love.

**If someone says, "I love God," and hates his brother, he is a liar; for he who does not love his brother whom he has seen, how can he love God whom he has not seen? And this commandment we have from Him: that he who loves God *must* love his brother also.**

a. **If someone says, "I love God"**: It is often easier for someone to proclaim his love for God, because that regards a private relationship with an invisible God. But John rightly insists that our claim of loving God is false if we do not also love our brother, and that this love must be seen.

    i. One may be a spiritual dwarf because one lacks love. One may know the Word, may never miss a service, may pray fervently, and may demonstrate gifts of the Spirit. Yet in it all, that one may be like Cain, offering to God the fruit of his hands and not the fruit of the Spirit.

b. **If someone says, "I love God," and hates his brother, he is a liar**: By this crucial measure, Jesus said the world could measure our status as disciples by the measure of our love for one another. *By this all will know that you are My disciples, if you have love for one another* (John 13:35).

i. There is a difference between the love of man, and divine love. "These verses are the equivalent of saying that a person cannot practice *agape*-love unless he can first practice *philia*-love." (Boice)

c. **And this commandment we have from Him**: We have a **commandment** to love. Though love springs forth from our abiding relationship with God and comes from our being born of Him, there is also an essential aspect of our *will* involved. We are therefore *commanded* to love our brother in Christ.

i. Being born of God and abiding with Him give us the ability to love; but it is a choice of our will to draw upon that resource and give it out to others. Therefore we are given a command to love, **that he who loves God *must* love his brother also**.

ii. Because of this, the excuse "I just can't love that person" (or other such excuses) is invalid. If we are born of Him and are abiding in Him then the resources for love are there. It is up to us to respond to His command with our will and whole being.

d. **He who loves God must love his brother also**: We can also *learn* how to love God by loving people. One might say, "I want to love God more; I want to grow in my love for Him. But how can I love a God who is invisible?" God would say to us, "Learn to love Me, Whom you cannot see, by loving My children, whom you can see."

i. Jesus said in Matthew 5:23-24, *Therefore if you bring your gift to the altar, and there remember that your brother has something against you, leave your gift there before the altar, and go your way. First be reconciled to your brother, and then come and offer your gift*. God is more pleased when you get it right with your brother, than if you bring Him a sacrifice of praise or resources.

# 1 John 5 - Born of God and Believing in the Son of God

A. Being born of God.

1. (1) Being born of God is the source of love.

**Whoever believes that Jesus is the Christ is born of God, and everyone who loves Him who begot also loves him who is begotten of Him.**

a. **Whoever believes that Jesus is the Christ is born of God**: John has often mentioned being **born of God** (as in 1 John 2:29, 3:9, and 4:7). Here he tells us *how* one is born of God: **whoever believes that Jesus is the Christ**. This means believing that Jesus is *his* Messiah, not just the Messiah in the generic sense.

i. John's great emphasis has been on love, but he never wants anyone to believe he *earns* salvation by loving others. We are **born of God** when we put our trust on Jesus and on His saving work in our lives.

ii. We also understand that John was not talking about a mere intellectual assent to Jesus being Messiah (as even the demons might have, as described in James 2:19). Instead, he means a trust in and reliance on Jesus as Messiah.

iii. Additionally, John makes it plain we must believe **Jesus *is* the Christ**. There are many, of a new-age sort of thinking, who believe Jesus *had* the "Christ-spirit" – as they claim also Confucius, Mohammed, Buddha and certain moderns did. But we would never say Jesus "has" the Christ – **Jesus *is* the Christ**.

b. **Everyone who loves Him who begot also loves him who is begotten of Him**: Being born of God also has these two effects. It is assumed that we will love God (**Him who begot us**), because we are born again into His family. But it is also assumed that we will love others who are **begotten of Him** - our brothers and sisters in Christ.

i. This is the common ground of Christians - not race, not class, not culture, not language, nor any other thing except for a common birth in Jesus Christ, and the common Lordship of Jesus.

ii. To love all others in the family of God means that you do not limit your love to your own denomination or group, to your own social or financial status, to your own race, to your own political perspective, or to your own exact theological persuasion. If any of these things mean more to us than our common salvation, and the common Lordship of Jesus Christ, then something is very wrong.

iii. Parents are exasperated, and even disgusted, when they see their children fight and seem to hate one another. How must God feel when He sees His children fight among themselves?

2. (2-3) The demonstration of God's love.

**By this we know that we love the children of God, when we love God and keep His commandments. For this is the love of God, that we keep His commandments. And His commandments are not burdensome.**

a. **By this we know that we love the children of God**: Just as much as our love for the people of God reflects our love for God (as expressed in 1 John 3:10, 17), so our love and obedience to God is a demonstration of love to the body of Christ.

i. It is sometimes said that the best thing a father can do for his children is to love his wife and their mother. Even so, the first way for a child of God to love his brothers and sisters in Christ is to love God and to obey Him. And, if you love the parent, you will love the child. It all works together.

b. **When we love God and keep His commandments**: A Christian who does not **love God** or **keep His commandments** is of little effective use in the body of Christ. This is true even though he or she might be involved in much ministry and hold an official position of service in the church.

i. When our love and obedience for God grows cold, we do not only harm ourselves - we harm our brothers and sisters also. The damage is done, at the very least, because we are a "drag" on the spiritual progress of God's people.

ii. If we will not love and obey God for our own sake, then we should at least do it out of love for others.

c. **For this is the love of God, that we keep His commandments**: To love God is also to **keep His commandments**. The one who says he loves God, yet walks in a lifestyle of conscious disobedience is like the believer who says he walks in fellowship with God, yet walks in darkness (as in 1 John 1:6) - he is lying.

i. Surely, John had the words of Jesus in mind: *If you love Me, keep My commandments* (John 14:15).

ii. Simply, love for God will show itself in obedience. "Christians frequently attempt to turn love for God into a mushy emotional experience, but John does not allow this in his epistle." (Boice)

d. **His commandments are not burdensome**: Some Christians feel very burdened by the commandments of God, yet John insists that they are **not burdensome**.

i. **His commandments are not burdensome** when we see how wise and good the commandments of God are. They are gifts from Him to show us the best and most fulfilling life possible. God's commands are like the "manufacture's handbook" for life; He tells us what to do because He knows how we work best. God's commands are not given to bind or to pain us, or because God is like an irritated old man.

ii. **His commandments are not burdensome** because when we are born again, we are given new hearts – hearts which by instinct wish to please God. As part of the New Covenant, the law of God has been written on the heart of every believer (Jeremiah 31:33).

iii. **His commandments are not burdensome** when we compare them to the religious rules men make up. John is not trying to say obedience is an easy thing. If that were so, then it would be easy for us to not sin, and John has already acknowledged that we all do sin (1 John 1:8). John is thinking of the contrast Jesus made between the religious requirements of the religious leaders of His day, and the simplicity of loving God and following Him. Jesus said all the rules and regulations of the Scribes and Pharisees were as *heavy burdens* (Matthew 23:4). In contrast, Jesus said of Himself, *My yoke is easy and My burden is light* (Matthew 11:30). Instead of the burdensome requirement to keep hundreds of little rules and regulations, Jesus simply says to us, *"Love Me and love my people, and you will walk in obedience."*

iv. **His commandments are not burdensome** when we really love God. When we love God, we will *want* to obey Him and please Him. When you love someone, it seems little trouble to go to a lot of difficulty to help or please that person. You enjoy doing it, though if you had to do it for an enemy, you would be complaining all the time. Just as the seven years of Jacob's service for Laban *seemed only a few days to him because of the love he had for her* (Genesis 29:18), so obeying God's commands does not seem a burden when we really love Him. An old proverb says, "Love feels no loads."

3. (4-5) Being born of God is the source of victory.

**For whatever is born of God overcomes the world. And this is the victory that has overcome the world - our faith. Who is he who overcomes the world, but he who believes that Jesus is the Son of God?**

a. **Whatever is born of God overcomes the world**: John begins with a principle that is so simple, yet so powerful - if we are **born of God**, we will overcome the world. The idea that anything born of God could be defeated by this world was strange to John and it should be strange to us.

b. **This is the victory that has overcome the world; our faith**: Since believing on Him is the key to being born of God (1 John 5:1), the key to victory is **faith**, not only an initial, "come-to-the-altar-and-get-saved" faith, but a consistently abiding faith, an ongoing reliance and trust upon Jesus Christ.

i. John repeats the thought with the words, **Who is he who overcomes the world, but he who believes that Jesus is the Son of God?** The life of *abiding faith and trust* in Jesus Christ is the life that overcomes the pressures and temptations of the world.

ii. Knowing who Jesus is – not just as a matter of facts or information, but as food for life - "fills the soul with so great things concerning him . . . as to easily turn this world into a contemptible shadow, and deprive it of all its former power over us." (Poole)

c. **Who is he who overcomes the world**: This tells us we overcome primarily because of *who we are* in Christ, not because of *what we do*. We overcome because we are **born of God**, and we are born of God because we **believe that Jesus is the Son of God** - again, not in a mere intellectual sense, but we put our lives on the fact that Jesus is the Son of God *for us*.

i. "Look at any Greek lexicon you like, and you will find that the word [faith or believe] does not merely mean to believe, but to trust, to confide in, to commit to, entrust with, and so forth; the very marrow of the meaning of faith is confidence in, reliance upon." (Spurgeon)

ii. How is it we can become world-overcomers in Jesus?

- *In the world you will have tribulation; but be of good cheer, I have overcome the world* (John 16:33). Because Jesus has overcome the world, as we abide in Him, we are overcomers in Jesus.

- John said of those who were growing in their walk with Jesus, *you have overcome the wicked one* (1 John 2:13-14). As we walk with Jesus and grow in that walk, we will overcome our spiritual enemies.

- Overcomers have a special place in the world to come. Jesus promised *To him who overcomes I will grant to sit with Me on My throne, as I also overcame and sat down with My Father on His throne* (Revelation 3:21).

- Overcomers overcome because the blood of Jesus overcomes Satan's accusations, the word of their testimony overcomes Satan's deceptions, and loving not their lives overcomes Satan's violence (Revelation 12:11).

B. The source of our relationship with God: Jesus Christ.

1. (6-8) Precisely identifying who **Jesus**, the **Son of God** is, the One on Whom we must believe.

**This is He who came by water and blood - Jesus Christ; not only by water, but by water and blood. And it is the Spirit who bears witness, because the Spirit is truth. For there are three that bear witness in heaven: the Father, the Word, and the Holy Spirit; and these three are one. And there are three that bear witness on earth: the Spirit, the water, and the blood; and these three agree as one.**

a. **He who came by water and blood**: John makes it clear that the Jesus he speaks of is not the Gnostic, "phantom" Jesus who was so holy that He had nothing to do with this world. The Jesus we must believe on is the Jesus who **came by water and blood**; the Jesus who was part of a real, material, flesh-and-blood earth.

i. John returns to a theme he started with in the beginning of the letter: the real, historical foundation for our trust in Jesus Christ. In 1 John 1:1-3 the emphasis was on what was *seen* and *heard* and *looked upon* and *handled* – real stuff, real people, real things. Just like water and blood are real, so was the coming of the Son of God, Jesus Christ.

b. **He who came by water and blood**: Through the centuries, there have been many different ideas about exactly what John meant by this phrase. "This is the most perplexing passage in the Epistle and one of the most perplexing in the New Testament." (Plummer, cited in Boice)

i. Some believe that **water** speaks of *our own baptism*, and **blood** speaks of *receiving communion*, and that John writes of how Jesus comes to us in the two Christian sacraments of baptism and communion (Luther and Calvin had this idea). Yet, if this is the case, it doesn't add up with the historical perspective John had when he wrote "*came* **by water and blood.**" He seems to write of something that happened in the past, not something that is ongoing.

ii. Others (such as Augustine) believe the **water and blood** describes the water and blood which flowed from Jesus' side when He was stabbed with a spear on the cross: *But one of the soldiers pierced His side with a spear, and immediately blood and water came out* (John 19:34). This was an important event to the Apostle John because immediately after this description of water and blood, he added in his gospel: *And he who has seen has testified, and his testimony is true; and he knows that he is telling the truth, so that you may believe* (John 19:35). Yet, if this was John's meaning, it is a little unclear how it can be said that Jesus *came* **by water and blood**.

iii. Still others believe the **water** spoke of Jesus' first birth, being born of the "waters of the womb," and **blood** speaks of His death. If this is the case, John would be essentially writing, "Jesus was born like a man and died like a man. He was completely human, not some super-spiritual being who had no real contact with the material world." The Gnostics in John's day thought of Jesus as just such a super-spiritual being.

c. **He who came by water and blood**: Probably the best explanation (though there are good points to some of the other ideas) is the oldest recorded Christian understanding of this passage (first recorded by the ancient Christian Tertullian). Most likely, John means the **water** of Jesus' baptism, and the **blood** of His crucifixion.

i. When Jesus was baptized, He was not baptized in repentance for His own sin (He had none), but because He wanted to completely identify with sinful humanity. When He **came by water**, it was His way of saying, "I am one of you."

ii. When Jesus died on the cross, He did not die because He had to (death could have no power over Him), but He laid down His life to identify with sinful humanity and to save us from our sin. When He **came by . . . blood** it was so that He could stand in our place as a guilty sinner, and to take the punishment our sin deserved.

iii. This explanation also connects best with what Jesus said in John 3:5: *Most assuredly, I say to you, unless one is born of water and the Spirit, he cannot enter the kingdom of God.* The being *born of water* in this passage speaks of the cleansing waters of baptism.

d. **He who came by water and blood**: Some taught (and still teach) that Jesus received the "Christ Spirit" at His baptism, and the "Christ Spirit" left Jesus before He died on the cross (for them, it is unthinkable that God could hang on a cross). But John insisted that Jesus did not only come by the *water* of baptism, but also by the **blood** of the cross. He was just as much the Son of God on the cross as He was when the Father declared, *You are My beloved Son; in You I am well pleased* (Luke 3:22) at the baptism of Jesus.

> i. We may find it difficult to relate to this ancient manner of trying avoid the offense of the cross by saying, "It really wasn't the Son of God who hung on the cross." But in our modern age we have our own ways of trying to avoid the offense of the cross. Some deny Jesus was God at all, and just think of Him as a "noble martyr." Some trivialize the cross, making it a mere ornament in jewelry and pop fashion trends. Others replace the cross with a self-help, self-esteem gospel of psychology, or use a crossless evangelism.

e. **It is the Spirit who bears witness, because the Spirit is truth**: The Holy Spirit also bears witness to the true person of Jesus, even as Jesus promised He would (*He will testify of Me . . . He will glorify Me, for He will take of what is Mine and declare it to you* [John 15:26 and 16:14]). The consistent message of the Holy Spirit to us is, "Here is Jesus."

> i. "A priest was always ordained by sacrificial blood, cleansing water, and oil that spoke of the anointing of the Holy Spirit. So Jesus also had these three witnesses to His priestly ministry." (Spurgeon)

f. **The Spirit, the water, and the blood**: These are all consistent witnesses in telling us who Jesus is. We can know that **these three agree as one**. It isn't as if the Spirit tells us one thing, the water another, and the blood says something else. Jesus' life, death, and the Spirit all tell us who Jesus is, and they tell us it in agreement.

2. A few words on this text, regarding the notes in the margins or footnotes of many Bibles regarding 1 John 5:7-8.

a. The New King James Bible makes a marginal note on 1 John 5:7-8, stating that the words **in heaven: the Father, the Word, and the Holy Spirit; and these three are one. And there are three that bear witness on the earth** are words that are not included in the vast majority of New Testament Greek manuscripts.

> i. The words in question occur in no Greek manuscript until the fourteenth century, except for one eleventh century and one twelfth century manuscript in which they have been added to the margin by another hand.

> ii. In the first few hundred years of Christianity, there were many theological debates regarding the exact nature and understanding of the Trinity. In all of those debates, *no one* ever once quoted these words in question from 1 John 5:7-8. If they were originally written by John, it seems *very* strange that no early Christian would have quoted them. In

fact, though none of the ancient Christians quote from this verse, several of them do quote from 1 John 5:6 and 1 John 5:8. Why skip verse seven, especially if it is such a great statement of the Trinity?

iii. In all ancient translations – Syriac, Arabic, Ethiopian, Coptic, Sahidic, Armenian, Slavonian, and so forth, this disputed passage is not included. Only in the Latin Vulgate does it appear.

b. It is probably best to regard these words as the work of an over-zealous copyist who thought that the New Testament needed a little help with the doctrine of the Trinity, and he figured this was a good place to do it. Or perhaps the words just started as notes written in the margin of a manuscript, but the next person who copied the manuscript thought they must belong in the text itself.

i. While there is no explicit statement of the Trinity in the statement (such as this), it is woven into the fabric of the New Testament - we find the Father, Son, and Holy Spirit working together as equal, yet distinct Persons (Matthew 3:16-17; 28:19; Luke 1:35; John 1:33-34 14:16, 26; 16:13-15; 20:21-22; Acts 2:33-38; Romans 15:16; 2 Corinthians 1:21-22; 13:14; Galatians 4:6; Ephesians 3:14-16; 4:4-6; 1 Peter 1:2).

c. How did these words ever get included, if they are not in any ancient Greek manuscripts? The words were included in ancient Latin versions of the Bible, and in the year 1520, a great scholar named Erasmus produced a new, accurate edition of the Bible in ancient Greek. When people studied Erasmus' Bible, and compared it to the Latin version, they noticed he left out this passage, and they criticized him for it. When he was criticized, Erasmus said, "You won't find these words in any ancient Greek manuscript. If you find me one Greek manuscript with these words in them, I'll include it in my next printing." Someone "discovered" a manuscript with the words in them, but it wasn't an ancient manuscript at all. Erasmus knew this, but had already promised to add the words if someone found a manuscript with the words, so he reluctantly added the words in his 1522 edition. However, he also added a footnote, saying he thought that the new Greek manuscript had been written on purpose, just to embarrass him. That manuscript (*Codex Montfortii*) is on display in the library of Trinity College, Dublin.

i. This passage is called the "Johannine Comma" (or mistakenly, "Johannian Comma"), and is in only three Greek manuscripts. The *Codex Guelpherbytanus* was written in the seventeenth century. We know this manuscript is from the seventeenth century because it contains a quote from a book written in the seventeenth century. The *Codex Ravianus* or *Berolinensis*, which is a copy of a text printed in 1514. We know it was copied from that text because it repeats the same typographical mistakes the 1514 text has. The third manuscript is the one "discovered" in the days of Erasmus, the *Codex Montfortii*.

ii. Since the Greek text of the New Testament that Erasmus printed became one of the Greek texts used to make the King James Bible, these added words became part of the King James Bible.

d. Passages like this give us no reason to fear that our New Testaments are unreliable. In the entire New Testament, there are only 50 passages which have any sort of question regarding the reliability of the text, and none of those are the sole foundation for any Christian doctrine or belief. If 50 passages sound like a lot, see it this way: no more than one-one thousandth of the text is in question at all.

i. In addition, when such a passage like this is inserted, the textual evidence from the manuscripts makes it stick out like a sore thumb. This gives us assurance, not doubt.

ii. Evangelical Christians may not know much about these passages, but many religious people who don't believe the Trinity (such as a Jehovah's Witness) do know the textual issues around this passage. Therefore, if you bring up this verse to support your position, they will show you how this passage doesn't belong in the Bible. It may get some thinking, "Well, maybe the Trinity isn't true. Maybe Jesus isn't God. Maybe it's just the invention of people who would try to change the Bible." This can do some real damage.

iii. So a passage like this also warns us that when it comes to such matters, God doesn't need our help. The New Testament is fine just like God inspired it. It doesn't need our improvements. Though the teaching of these added words is true, they shouldn't be here, because we should not add our words to the Bible and claim they are God's words.

e. The text of 1 John 5:7-8 should more accurately read: **For there are three that bear witness: the Spirit, the water, and the blood; and these three agree as one.**

3. (9-10) The witness of men and the witness of God.

**If we receive the witness of men, the witness of God is greater; for this is the witness of God which He has testified of His Son. He who believes in the Son of God has the witness in himself; he who does not believe God has made Him a liar, because he has not believed the testimony that God has given of His Son.**

a. **If we receive the witness of men, the witness of God is greater**: Everybody, everyday, receives the witness of men regarding various things. Therefore, we should have much more confidence in the witness of God when He tells us who Jesus is.

> i. John does not want us to believe with blind faith. Instead, our faith is to be based on reliable testimony. And we have the most reliable testimony possible, **the witness of God**.

b. **He who believes in the Son of God has the witness in himself**: When we believe on Jesus, we receive the Holy Spirit as an inner confirmation of our standing before God. Romans 8:16 puts it like this: *The Spirit Himself bears witness with our Spirit that we are children of God.*

c. **He who does not believe God has made Him a liar**: When we refuse to believe on Jesus, we reject **the testimony God has given of His Son**. Therefore, we call God a liar with our unbelief.

> i. John here exposes the great sin of unbelief. Most everyone who refuses to believe God (in the full sense of the word *believe*) doesn't *intend* to call God a liar. But they do it nonetheless. "The great sin of not believing in the Lord Jesus Christ is often spoken of very lightly and in a very trifling spirit, as though it were scarcely any sin at all; yet, according to my text, and, indeed, according to the whole tenor of the Scriptures, unbelief is the giving of God the lie, and what can be worse?" (Spurgeon)
>
> ii. What if one says, "Well, I want to believe, but I *can't*." Spurgeon answers such a one: "Hearken, O unbeliever, you have said, 'I cannot believe,' but it would be more honest if you had said, 'I *will* not believe.' The mischief lies there. Your unbelief is your fault, not your misfortune. It is a disease, but it is also a crime: it is a terrible source of misery to you, but it is justly so, for it is an atrocious offense against the God of truth."
>
> iii. What if one says, "Well, I'm trying to believe, and I'll keep on trying." Spurgeon speaks to this heart: "Did I not hear some one say, 'Ah, sir, I have been *trying to believe* for years.' Terrible words! They make the case still worse. Imagine that after I had made a statement, a man should declare that he did not believe me, in fact, he could not believe me though he would like to do so. I should feel aggrieved certainly; but it would make matters worse if he added, 'In fact I have been for years trying to believe you, and I cannot do it.' What does he mean by that? What can he mean but that I am so incorrigibly false, and such a confirmed liar, that though he would like to give me some credit, he really cannot do it? With all the effort he can make in my

favour, he finds it quite beyond his power to believe me? Now, a man who says, 'I have been trying to believe in God,' in reality says just that with regard to the Most High . . . The talk about trying to believe is a mere pretence. But whether pretence or no, let me remind you that there is no text in the Bible which says, 'Try and believe,' but it says 'Believe in the Lord Jesus Christ.' He is the Son of God, he has proved it by his miracles, he died to save sinners, therefore trust him; he deserves implicit trust and child-like confidence. Will you refuse him these? Then you have maligned his character and given him the lie."

iv. Such rejection of God's testimony over time can lead to a place where a person is permanently hardened against God, to the place where they may be one who *blasphemes against the Holy Spirit*, as Jesus warned in Mark 3:28-29. What hope can there be for the one who persists in hearing what God says, and calling Him a **liar**?

4. (11-13) Assurance of life in the Son.

**And this is the testimony: that God has given us eternal life, and this life is in His Son. He who has the Son has life; he who does not have the Son of God does not have life. These things I have written to you who believe in the name of the Son of God, that you may know that you have eternal life, and that you may *continue to* believe in the name of the Son of God.**

a. **And this is the testimony**: John, in the previous verse, just told us how serious the matter of receiving the testimony of God is. Now he will tell us *what* this **testimony** is.

b. **That God has given us eternal life, and this life is in His Son**: This is God's essential message to man; that eternal life is a gift from God, received in Jesus Christ. **He who has the Son has life; he who does not have the Son of God does not have life**. It is all about Jesus, and living in Jesus is the evidence of eternal life.

i. "It is vain to expect eternal glory, if we have not Christ in our heart. The indwelling Christ gives both a title to it, and a meetness for it. This is God's record. Let no man deceive himself here. An *indwelling Christ* and GLORY; *no indwelling Christ*, NO glory. God's record must stand." (Clarke)

c. **These things I have written to you who believe . . . that you may know that you have eternal life**: In stating the message so plainly, John hopes to persuade us to believe. Even if we already believe, he wants us to **know that you have eternal life**, so we can have this assurance, and so that **you may continue to believe**.

i. The need to hear the simple gospel of salvation in Jesus Christ does not end once one embraces the gospel. We benefit by it, are assured by it, and are helped to continue in it as we hear it and embrace it over and over again.

d. **That you may know that you have eternal life**: John's confidence is impressive. He wants us **to** *know* **that** we **have eternal life**. We can only *know* this if our salvation rests in Jesus and not in our own performance. If it depends on me, then on a good day I'm saved and on a bad day, I don't really know. But if it depends on what Jesus has done for me, then I can **know**.

C. Help for the praying Christian.

1. (14-15) Confidence in prayer.

**Now this is the confidence that we have in Him, that if we ask anything according to His will, He hears us. And if we know that He hears us, whatever we ask, we know that we have the petitions that we have asked of Him.**

a. **This is the confidence that we have in Him**: John has developed the idea of **confidence in Him**. In the previous verse, 1 John 5:13, he wrote *to you who believe in the name of the Son of God, that you may know you have eternal life*. Now, for those who *know* they *have eternal life*, John relates the idea of **confidence in Him** to prayer.

b. **If we ask anything according to His will, He hears us**: In this, we see the *purpose* of prayer and the secret of *power* in prayer. It is to **ask**; to ask **anything**; to ask anything **according to His will**; and once having so asked, to have the assurance that **He hears us**.

i. First, God would have us **ask** in prayer. Much prayer fails because it never *asks* for anything. God is a loving God, and a generous giver – He wants us to **ask** of Him.

ii. Secondly, God would have us **ask anything** in prayer. Not to imply that **anything** we ask for will be granted, but **anything** in the sense that we can and should pray about *everything*. God cares about our whole life, and nothing is too small or too big to pray about. As Paul wrote in Philippians 4:6: *Be anxious for nothing, but in everything by prayer and supplication, with thanksgiving, let your requests be made known to God.*

iii. Next, God would have us ask **according to His will**. It is easy for us to only be concerned with *our* will before God, and to have a fatalistic view regarding His will ("He will accomplish His will with or without my prayers anyway, won't He?"). But God wants us to see and discern His will through His Word, and to pray His will into action. When John wrote this, John may have had Jesus' own words in mind, which he recorded in John 15:7: *If you abide in Me, and My words abide in* *you, you will ask what you desire, and it shall be done for you.* When we *abide* in Jesus – living in Him, day by day – then our will becomes more and more aligned with His will, and we can *ask what you desire*, and more and more be asking **according to His will**. Then we see answered prayer.

iv. If something is God's will, why doesn't He just do it, apart from our prayers? Why would He wait to accomplish His will until we pray? Because God has appointed us to work with Him as 2 Corinthians 6:1 says: *as workers together with Him.* God wants us to work with Him, and that means bringing our will and agenda into alignment with His. He wants us to care about the things He cares about, and He wants us to care about them enough to pray passionately about them.

c. **We know that we have the petitions that we have asked of Him**: When we ask according to God's will, when we pray the promises of God, we have this confidence; and so pray with real and definite faith.

i. Prayer should be so much more than casting wishes to heaven. It is rooted in understanding God's will and promises according to His Word, and praying those promises into action. For each prayer request, we should mentally or vocally ask, "What possible reason do I have to think that God will answer this prayer?" We should be able to answer that question from His Word.

ii. The most powerful prayers in the Bible are always prayers which understand the will of God, and ask Him to perform it. We may be annoyed when one of our children says, "Daddy, this is what you promised, now please do it," but God is delighted when we pray His promises. It shows our will aligned with His, our dependence on Him, and that we take His Word seriously.

iii. It is not necessarily *wrong* to ask for something that God has not promised; but we then realize that we are not coming to God on the basis of a specific promise, and we don't have the confidence to **know that we have the petitions that we have asked of Him**.

2. (16-17) Praying for a sinning brother.

**If anyone sees his brother sinning a sin *which does* not *lead* to death, he will ask, and He will give him life for those who commit sin not *leading* to death. There is sin *leading* to death. I do not say that he should pray about that. All unrighteousness is sin, and there is sin not *leading* to death.**

a. **If anyone sees his brother sinning a sin . . . he will ask**: When we see a brother in sin, John tells us the first thing to do is to *pray* for that person. All too often, prayer is the *last* thing we do, or the *smallest* thing we do in regard to our brother having a difficult time.

b. **And He will give him life**: God promised to bless the prayer made on behalf of a brother in sin. Perhaps such prayers have special power before God because they are prayers in fulfillment of the command to love the brethren. Surely, we love each other best when we pray for each other.

c. **There is sin leading to death**: Because John wrote in context of a **brother**, it is wrong to see him meaning a sin leading to **spiritual** death; he probably meant a sin leading to the **physical** death of the believer.

i. This is a difficult concept, but we have an example of it in 1 Corinthians 11:27-30, where Paul says that among the Christians in Corinth, because of their disgraceful conduct at the Lord's Supper, some had died (*many are weak and sick among you, and many sleep*). This death came not as a condemning judgment, but as a corrective judgment (*But when we are judged, we are chastened by the Lord, that we may* not *be condemned with the world* [1 Corinthians 11:32]).

ii. Apparently, a believer *can* sin to the point where God believes it is just best to bring them home, probably because they have in some way compromised their testimony so significantly that they should just come on home to God.

iii. However, it is certainly presumptuous to think this about every case of an untimely death of a believer, or to use it as an enticement to suicide for the guilt-ridden Christian. Our lives are in God's hands, and if *He* sees fit to bring one of His children home, that is fine.

iv. Some believe that **brother** is used here in a very loose sense, and what John means by the **sin leading to death** is the blasphemy of the Holy Spirit, which is the willful, settled rejection of Jesus Christ. But this would be a curious use of the term **brother**, especially according to how John has already used **brother** in his own letter.

d. **I do not say that he should pray about that**: Apparently, when a Christian is being corrected in regard to a **sin leading to death**, there is no point in praying for his recovery or restoration - the situation is in God's hands alone.

e. **There is sin not leading to death**: John takes pains to recognize that not *every* sin leads to death in the manner he speaks of, though **all unrighteousness is sin**.

D. Protecting our relationship with God.

1. (18-19) Knowing who we are and who our enemies are.

**We know that whoever is born of God does not sin; but he who has been born of God keeps himself, and the wicked one does not touch him. We know that we are of God, and the whole world lies *under the sway of* the wicked one.**

a. **Whoever is born of God does not sin**: In the battle against sin, it is all-essential that we keep our minds set on who we are in Jesus Christ. If we are **born of Him**, we then have the resources to be free from habitual sin.

> i. John is repeating his idea from 1 John 3:6: *Whoever abides in Him does not sin*. The grammar in the original language makes it plain John is speaking of a settled, continued lifestyle of sin. John is not teaching here the possibility of sinless perfection. As Stott says, "The present tense in the Greek verb implied habit, continuity, unbroken sequence."

b. **He who has been born of God keeps himself, and the wicked one does not touch him**: If we are **born of Him** we then have a protection against the **wicked one**, a unique protection that does not belong to the one who is not **born of Him**. Knowing this gives us godly confidence in spiritual warfare.

> i. In verse 18, **himself** is more accurately *him*. What John probably means here is that *He* **who has been born of God** (that is, Jesus Christ) **keeps** *him* (that is, the believer). John means that we are kept by Jesus and protected from Satan by Him.

c. **Does not touch him**: The word **touch** here has the idea of *to attach one's self to*. John clearly says that the **wicked one** – Satan, or, by implication one of His demons - cannot attach himself to the one who is **born of Him**.

> i. What Greek scholars say about this word **touch**: The word is "stronger than *toucheth*; rather *graspeth, layeth hold of*" (Smith, in *Expositor's*). "It means to lay hold of or to grasp rather than a mere superficial touch." (Robertson)

> ii. The only other place in his writings where John uses this particular verb for **touch** is in John 20:17, where He literally tells Mary to *stop clinging to Me*. Because we are **born of Him**, Satan cannot attach himself to us, or cling to us, in the sense he can in the life of someone who is not **born of Him**.

d. **We know that we are of God**: If we are **born of Him**, we are set off from the world - we are no longer **under the sway of the wicked one**, though the **whole world** still is. Knowing this means we can be free to be what we are in Jesus and separate ourselves from the world system in rebellion against Him.

2. (20-21) Abide in Jesus and avoid idols.

**And we know that the Son of God has come and has given us an understanding, that we may know Him who is true; and we are in Him who is true, in His Son Jesus Christ. This is the true God and eternal life. Little children, keep yourselves from idols. Amen.**

a. **That we may know Him who is true, and we are in Him who is true, in His Son Jesus Christ**: In the conclusion of this letter, John returned to his major theme: fellowship with Jesus Christ. We must **know Him**, and the word John uses for **know** (*ginosko*) speaks of knowledge by *experience*. That is how Jesus wants us to know Him.

b. **Has given us an understanding**: The work of Jesus in us gives us **an understanding**, and the ability to **know Him**, and to be **in Him** - the abiding life of fellowship that John invited us to back in 1 John 1:3.

i. Significantly, this **understanding** must be **given**. We cannot attain it on our own. If God did not reveal Himself to us, we would never find Him. We know Him, and can know Him, because He has revealed Himself to us.

ii. More than any other way, God has revealed Himself to us by **Him who is true, in His Son Jesus Christ**. Jesus is the key and the focus of it all. We see the personality and character of God by looking at Jesus.

iii. **Him who is true** also reminds us of a theme John has had through the letter: the importance of true belief, of trusting in the true Jesus, not a made-up Jesus. The Jesus of the Bible is **Him who is true**, who is **His Son Jesus Christ**.

c. **This is the true God and eternal life**: Here John tells us who Jesus is. He was a man (as John declared in 1 John 1:1, 4:2, and 5:6), but He was not *only* a man. He was totally man and **the true God and eternal life**. John does not, and we can not, promote the humanity of Jesus over His deity, or His deity over His humanity. He is both: fully God and fully man.

i. John Stott says of the statement, **this is the true God and eternal life**: "This would be the most unequivocal statement of the deity of Jesus Christ in the New Testament, which the champions of orthodoxy were quick to exploit against the heresy of Arius." (Stott)

d. **Keep yourselves from idols**: This may seem like a strange way to end John's letter, but it fits in with the theme of a real, living relationship with God. The enemy to fellowship with God is *idolatry*: embracing a false god, or a false idea of the true God. John rightly closes with this warning, after having spent much of the book warning us against the dangers of the false Jesus many were teaching in his day (1 John 3:18-23; 4:1-3; 5:6-9).

i. We can only have a *real relationship* with the God who is *really there*! Idolatry, whether obvious (praying to a statue) or subtle (living for your career or someone other than God) will always choke out a *real relationship* with God, and damage our relationships with our brothers and sisters in Jesus. No wonder John ends with **keep yourselves from idols**; this is how we *protect* our relationship with God.

ii. In a great sermon in this last verse of John's letter, Charles Spurgeon first noted that John addressed **little children**.

- This is a title of deep affection.

- This is a title that indicates regeneration and family relation.

- This is a title that indicates humility.

- This is a title that indicates teachableness.

- This is a title that implies faith.

- This is a title that implies weakness.

iii. Then, Spurgeon noted that John gave a command: To **keep yourselves from idols**.

- This speaks against obvious, visible idols.

- This speaks against worshipping yourself. We can do this by overindulgence in food or drink, by laziness, or by too much concern about how we look or what we wear.

- This speaks against worshipping wealth.

- This speaks against worshipping some hobby or pursuit.

- This speaks against worshipping dear friends or relatives.

# 2 John - Walking In the Truth

*"This epistle is more remarkable for the spirit of Christian love which it breathes than for anything else. It contains scarcely anything that is not found in the preceding; and out of the thirteen verses there are at least eight which are found, either in so many words or in sentiment, precisely the same with those of the first epistle."* (Adam Clarke)

A. Greeting.

1. (1-2) To **the elect lady and her children**.

**THE ELDER, To the elect lady and her children, whom I love in truth, and not only I, but also all those who have known the truth, because of the truth which abides in us and will be with us forever.**

a. **The Elder**: The writer of this book identifies himself as **the Elder**. Presumably, his first readers knew exactly who he was, and from the earliest times, Christians have understood this was the Apostle John writing.

i. "John the apostle, who was now a very old man, generally supposed to be about ninety, and therefore uses the term presbyter or elder, not as the name of an *office*, but as designating his advanced age. He is allowed to have been the oldest of all the apostles, and to have been the only one who died a natural death." (Clarke)

b. **To the elect lady and her children**: Perhaps this was an individual Christian woman John wanted to warn and encourage by this letter. Or, the term might be a symbolic way of addressing this particular congregation.

i. "The phrase is, however, more likely to be a personification than a person - not the church at large but some local church over which the elder's jurisdiction was recognized, *her children* being the church's individual members." (Stott)

ii. "This appears to have been some noted person, whom both her singular piety, and rank in the world, made eminent, and capable of having great influence for the support of the Christian interest." (Poole)

iii. John probably did not name himself, **the elect lady** or **her children** by name because this was written during a time of persecution. Perhaps John didn't want to implicate anyone by name in a written letter. If the letter was intercepted and the authorities knew who it was written to by name, it might mean death for those persons.

c. **Whom I love in truth, and not only I**: Whomever **the elect lady** was, she was loved by all who **have known the truth**. If we know and love the truth, we will love those who also know and love the truth - **the truth which abides in us** also lives in others who know the truth.

i. We see John quite focused on the idea of truth, as he was in all of his writings. He used the word *truth* some thirty-seven times in his New Testament writings.

ii. This shows that what binds Christians together is not social compatibility or political compatibility or class compatibility. What binds us together is a common **truth**. This is why truth is important to Christians.

d. **Will be with us forever**: The truth does not change. The truth will be true **forever**, and we will have the truth forever in eternity. Many people today think that the truth changes from age to age and from generation to generation, but the Bible knows that the truth **will be with us forever**.

2. (3) John's salutation to his readers.

**Grace, mercy, *and* peace will be with you from God the Father and from the Lord Jesus Christ, the Son of the Father, in truth and love.**

a. **Grace, mercy, and peace**: John presents a slightly expanded version of the standard greeting in New Testament letters. He didn't just wish these for his readers; he confidently bestowed them by saying they **will be with you from God the Father**.

b. **In truth and love**: John can hardly write a verse without mentioning these two of his favorite topics. The **grace, mercy, and peace** God has for us are all given **in truth and love**. Apart from God's **truth and love**, we can never really have **grace, mercy, and peace**.

i. "What deep, sweet rhythm of meaning there is in the first three verses of this letter! One reads them over and over again. Oh, that the grace, mercy, and peace, may be with us, from God the Father, and from Jesus Christ, the Son of the Father, in truth and in love." (Meyer)

c. **The Son of the Father**: "The apostle still keeps in view the *miraculous conception* of Christ; a thing which the *Gnostics* absolutely denied; a doctrine which is at the ground work of our salvation."

B. How to walk.

1. (4) John's joy to find they are **walking in truth**.

**I rejoiced greatly that I have found** *some* **of your children walking in truth, as we received commandment from the Father.**

a. **I rejoiced greatly**: This is a pastor's heart - to know that his people are **walking in truth**. While **truth** is not the *only* concern of a pastor, it is a great concern; and it is a great comfort for a pastor to see those he loves and cares for **walking in truth**.

i. "The *children* mentioned here may either be *her own children*, or those *members of the Church* which were under her care, or some of *both*." (Clarke)

b. **I have found some of your children walking in truth**: John rejoiced because when God's people are **walking in truth**, they also abide in God. The same idea is expressed in 1 John 2:24: *Therefore let that abide in you which you heard from the beginning. If what you heard from the beginning abides in you, you also will abide in the Son and in the Father.* Truth is not only important for its own sake, but also our **walking in truth** shows we are walking with the Lord.

i. Trapp on the idea of **walking in the truth**: "Not taking a step or two, not breaking or leaping over the hedge to avoid a piece of foul way, but persisting in a Christian course, not starting aside to the right hand or the left."

2. (5) The commandment to love one another.

**And now I plead with you, lady, not as though I wrote a new commandment to you, but that which we have had from the beginning: that we love one another.**

a. **I plead with you, lady**: John was not too proud to beg on such an important matter - not when it came to something as vital in the Christian life as the **commandment** that we must **love one another**.

b. **Not as though I wrote a new commandment**: John knew this was nothing new to his readers (he repeated the theme all through 1 John and his gospel). Yet because it was so essential, it had to be repeated and used as a reminder.

c. **That we love one another**: The integrity of our Christian life can be measured by our love for one another (as in John 13:35 and 1 John 4:20-21).

3. (6) Showing the love of God.

**This is love, that we walk according to His commandments. This is the commandment, that as you have heard from the beginning, you should walk in it.**

a. **This is love, that we walk according to His commandments**: If we love God, we will obey His commandments. We do this not because we think His commandments are heavy burdens, but because we see that they are best for us. They are guides and gifts to us from God.

b. **Walk according to His commandments**: Real love will walk this way. Perhaps John warned against those who thought the only important thing in the Christian life was a vague love that had no heart for obedience.

> i. "Perhaps you fail to distinguish between love and the emotion of love. They are not the same. We may love without being directly conscious of love, or being able to estimate its strength and passion. Here is the solution to many of our questionings: They love who obey." (Meyer)

4. (7-9) A warning against the presence and dangers of false teachers.

**For many deceivers have gone out into the world who do not confess Jesus Christ *as* coming in the flesh. This is a deceiver and an antichrist. Look to yourselves, that we do not lose those things we worked for, but *that* we may receive a full reward. Whoever transgresses and does not abide in the doctrine of Christ does not have God. He who abides in the doctrine of Christ has both the Father and the Son.**

a. **Many deceivers have gone out into the world**: John was aware false teachers were a danger to the church in his day.

> i. "The immediate problem in [2 John] is that of traveling teachers or missionaries. According to Christian ethics all who thus traveled about were to be shown hospitality by Christians in the town to which they came." (Boice)

b. **This is a deceiver**: John mainly had in mind the danger in his own time, the danger of those who thought that the Jesus, being God, could have no *real* connection with the material world. They said that He only had an *apparent* connection with the material world.

> i. To combat this, John made a plain declaration: we must **confess Jesus Christ as coming in the flesh**. This means Jesus came as a real man in His first coming, but also means He will come as a human being – although glorified humanity, and that added to His eternal deity - a real flesh and blood Jesus will come again to the earth.

c. **This is a deceiver and an antichrist**: Against this false idea of Jesus, John insists those **who do not confess Jesus Christ as coming in the flesh** are the deceivers and have the spirit of the **antichrist**.

> i. John warned us against these antichrists in his first letter (1 John 2:18-23, 4:3). They are those who not only oppose Jesus, but also offer a substitute "Christ."

ii. This spirit of antichrist will one day find its ultimate fulfillment in *the Antichrist*, who will lead humanity in an end-times rebellion against God.

d. **Whoever transgresses and does not abide in the doctrine of Christ does not have God**: There is nothing noble, sincere, courageous, or admirable in a *false* Jesus. To deny the Biblical Jesus is *always* to reject the Father and the Son both. John here draws a critical line of truth, over which it is heresy to *transgress*.

i. In our own day, we must deal with modern denials of the Biblical Jesus with the same passion John did in his day. Today, with our "scholarly" denials of Jesus and the historical record of the Gospels, it is more important than ever to know who the true Jesus is according to the Bible and to love and serve the true Jesus.

ii. "To say *no* to God's way of revealing himself is to say *no* to God himself, for he will not let himself be known by men except on his own terms." (Marshall)

e. **Transgresses**: The word *transgresses* has the idea of "going beyond a boundary." We never go "beyond" the teaching of Jesus, of who He is and what He has done for us. Anyone who thinks we have or should go beyond what the Bible plainly says about Jesus *transgresses*.

i. "There is a true progress in the Christian life, but it is progress based upon a deeper knowledge of the historical, biblical Christ. Progress on any other ground may be called progress, but it is a progress that leaves God behind and is, therefore, not progress at all." (Boice)

ii. "When the teaching of the Bible needs to be supplemented by some 'key' to the Bible or by some new revelation, it is a sure sign that 'advanced' doctrine is being put forth." (Marshall)

f. **Look to yourselves, that we do not lose those things we worked for**: To depart from the true Jesus means you put yourself in jeopardy to lose the things the apostles and other faithful saints **worked for**. This shows us that it isn't enough for us to start out right, we must finish in faith to **receive a full reward**.

5. (10-11) Instructions for dealing with the false teachers.

**If anyone comes to you and does not bring this doctrine, do not receive him into your house nor greet him; for he who greets him shares in his evil deeds.**

a. **If anyone comes to you and does not bring this doctrine**: If someone comes to us, denying the true doctrine of Jesus, and promoting a false doctrine of Jesus, John says we should give no hospitality, no aid, to the ones who promote their own false version of Jesus. To do so is to share **in his evil deeds**.

> i. "The words mean, according to the eastern use of them, 'Have no religious connection with him, nor act towards him so as to induce others to believe you acknowledge him as a brother.' " (Clarke)

> ii. "Suppose the visiting teacher claimed to be a Christian missionary or even a prophet but taught what was clearly false doctrine. Hospitality would demand that he be provided for, but to do so would seem to be participation in the spread of his false teachings. Should he be received or not?" (Boice)

b. **He who greets him:** John means **greets** in a much more involved context than our own. In that culture, it meant to show hospitality and give aid. Yet, for the weak or unskilled believer, it is best if they do not even *greet* (in the sense of speaking to) those who promote a false Jesus (like the Mormons or Jehovah's Witnesses).

> i. These words sound severe, but John has not lost his love. We must consider these three points:

> - John is not talking about *all* error, but only error which *masquerades* as true Christianity.
>
> - John is not talking about all who *hold* the error which masquerades as true Christianity, but about those who *teach* those errors which masquerade as true Christianity.
>
> - John is not talking about all *teachers* who err, but those who err in the most *fundamental* truths, and those who are active in spreading those fundamental errors.

> ii. This does not mean that we should have nothing to do with those who are caught by the cults. As John indicates, we should make a distinction between those who *teach* these Christ-denying doctrines (those who **bring** this doctrine) and those who merely *believe* the doctrines without trying to spread them.

c. **Do not receive him into your house nor greet him**: This may also be translated *do not receive him into the house*. John may be referring most specifically to not allowing these heretical teachers to come into **the house** where Christians meet together.

> i. "Perhaps, therefore, it is not private hospitality which John is forbidding so much as an official welcome into the congregation, with the opportunity this would afford to the false teacher to propagate his errors." (Stott)

ii. "We see how such [false] teachers were treated in the apostolic Church. They held no communion with them; afforded them no support, as *teachers*; but *did not persecute* them." (Clarke)

d. **Shares in his evil deeds**: We are defined by what we *reject* as much as by what we *accept*. In this, some are so *open minded* that they are *empty headed*. It is wise to keep an open mind on many things; but one would never keep an open mind about which poisons a person might try. You may say *yes* to all the right things; but one must also say *no* to what is false and evil. We need to become good at rejecting what should be rejected.

i. "They were persons who claimed to be leaders; they were advanced thinkers, they were progressive. The Gnostic teachers of the time were claiming that while the gospel of the historic Jesus might be all very well for unenlightened people, they had a profounder knowledge. Such were to receive no hospitality." (Morgan)

ii. In the late 19th Century, the rise of theological liberalism brought forth generations of Christian pastors, leaders, and theologians who denied many of the fundamentals of Biblical Christianity. Though it was a broad and varied movement, at its root theological liberalism thought that Christianity had to re-evaluate all its doctrines in the light of modern science, philosophy, and thinking. They rejected the idea that a doctrine was true simply because the Bible taught it; it also had to be proved true by reason and experience. They believed that the Bible was not an inspired message from a real God, but the work of men who were limited by the ignorance and superstitions of their time. For them, the Bible was not either inspired or supernatural. The importance of the Bible and its message was not in its literal or historical truth, but in its changing spiritual message.

C. Conclusion.

1. (12) John anticipates a future visit.

**Having many things to write to you, I did not wish *to do so* with paper and ink; but I hope to come to you and speak face to face, that our joy may be full.**

a. **I hope to come to you and speak face to face**: We must generally sympathize with John's preference for personal, face to face communication rather than the writing of letters - though we are thankful for this letter.

2. (13) Conclusion.

**The children of your elect sister greet you. Amen.**

a. **The children of your elect sister**: Telling us that the *elect lady* (2 John 1) has an **elect sister**, and that they both have **children** does little to identify with certainty who John is writing to. Perhaps all it tells us is that if John used the term *elect lady* as a symbol for the church, he used it rather loosely (saying that she has a sister and children). The most likely idea is that the *elect lady* (a particular church) had an **elect sister** – other "sister" churches from which John brings a greeting.

b. **The children of your elect sister**: This last reference to the **elect sister** and her **children** remind us that though we must be on guard against false teachers, the true followers of Jesus are more than just our group. If we allow our desire to defend the truth to make us unloving and intolerant, Satan has won a great victory.

# 3 John - Following Good Examples

"But it has been the lot both of the *minor prophets* and the *minor epistles* to be generally neglected; for with many readers *bulk* is every thing; and, no *magnitude*, no goodness." (Adam Clarke, on the shorter books of the Bible)

A. Greeting and introduction.

1. (1) The writer and the reader.

**THE ELDER, To the beloved Gaius, whom I love in truth.**

> a. **The Elder**: The writer of this book identifies himself simply as **the Elder**. Presumably, the first readers knew who this was, and from the earliest times, Christians have understood that this was the Apostle John writing, the same John who wrote the Gospel of John, 1 and 2 John, and the Book of Revelation.

> > i. Perhaps he does not directly refer to himself for the same reason he does not directly refer to his readers in 2 John - the threat of persecution may be making direct reference unwise; and of course, unnecessary.

> b. **To the beloved Gaius**: We don't know if this specific **Gaius** is connected with the other men by this name mentioned in the New Testament (Acts 19:29, 20:4; 1 Corinthians 1:14; Romans 16:23).

> > i. The identification is difficult because **Gaius** was a very common name in the Roman Empire.

2. (2-4) A blessing for faithful **Gaius**.

**Beloved, I pray that you may prosper in all things and be in health, just as your soul prospers. For I rejoiced greatly when brethren came and testified of the truth *that is* in you, just as you walk in the truth. I have no greater joy than to hear that my children walk in truth.**

> a. **Beloved, I pray that you may prosper in all things**: The word for **prosper** literally means "to have a good journey." It metaphorically means to succeed or prosper. It is like saying, "I hope things go well for you."

i. "Both verbs [for **prosper** and **be in health**] belonged to the every-day language of letter writing" (Stott). This phrase as so common that sometimes it was condensed into only initials, and everyone knew what the writer meant just from the initials.

ii. The abbreviation used in Latin was SVBEEV, meaning *Si vales, bene est; ego valeo* – "If you are well, it is good; I am well."

b. **I pray that you may prosper in all things and be in health, just as your soul prospers**: John used this common phrase in his sending of best wishes and blessings to **Gaius**. Some have wrongly taken this as a guarantee of perpetual wealth and perfect health for the Christian.

i. Of course, we should *always* remember that God wants our best and plans only good for us. Often present material prosperity and physical health are part of that good He has for us - and this prosperity and health are absolutely promised as the *ultimate* destiny of all believers.

ii. Yet, for the present time, God may - according to His all-wise plan - use a lack of material prosperity and physical health to promote greater prosperity and health in the scale of eternity.

iii. Nevertheless, *some* live in poverty and disease simply because they do not seek God's best, follow God's principles, and walk in faith. As well, there are *some others* who say we should use God's general promises of blessing as a way to indulge a carnal desire for ease, comfort, and luxury.

c. **Just as your soul prospers**: John here made an analogy between the condition of our health and the condition of our soul. Many Christians would be desperately ill if their physical health was instantly in the same state as their spiritual health.

d. **I have no greater joy than to hear that my children walk in truth**: John's goodwill towards **Gaius** came from his understanding that he walked in the truth. Nothing pleased John more than to know that his **children walk in truth**.

i. John knew that Gaius walked in truth because **brethren came and testified of the truth that** was in Gaius. His walk of truth was noticed by others, and they could talk about it because they saw it.

e. **That my children walk in truth**: This means more than living with correct doctrine. "What is it to 'walk in truth'? It is not walking in *the* truth, or else some would suppose it meant that John was overjoyed because they were sound in doctrine, and cared little for anything else. His joyous survey did include their orthodoxy in creed, but it reached far beyond." (Spurgeon)

i. To **walk in truth** means to walk consistent with the truth you believe. If you believe that you are fallen, then walk wary of your fallenness. If you believe you are a child of God, then walk like a child of heaven. If you believe you are forgiven, then walk like a forgiven person.

ii. To **walk in truth** means to walk in a way that is real and genuine, without any phoniness or concealment.

B. Learning from good and bad examples.

1. (5-8) Gaius: A good example.

**Beloved, you do faithfully whatever you do for the brethren and for strangers, who have borne witness of your love before the church. *If you send them forward on their journey in a manner worthy of God, you will do well, because they went forth for His name's sake, taking nothing from the Gentiles. We therefore ought to receive such, that we may become fellow workers for the truth.***

a. **You do faithfully whatever you do for the brethren and for strangers**: John praised Gaius for his hospitality. This may seem somewhat trivial to us, but it is not to God. This is a practical outworking of the essential command to love one another; it is love in action.

i. This was a great compliment: **you do faithfully whatever you do.** Whatever God gives us to do, we should do it **faithfully**. Jesus said that when we see Him face to face some will hear the words, *well done, good and faithful servant; you were faithful over a few things, I will make you ruler over many things. Enter into the joy of your lord* (Matthew 25:21). Of the good servant, it is said he was *faithful.*

b. **Send them forward on their journey in a manner worthy of God**: In that day, Christian travelers in general and itinerant ministers in particular were greatly dependent upon the hospitality of other Christians. John knew that when Christians assist those who contend for the truth, they become **fellow workers for the truth**.

i. The reward for these support people is the same as those who are out on the front lines. 1 Samuel 30:21-25 shows this principle, where the spoils are distributed equally among those who fought and those who supported. King David understood that the supply lines were just as vital as the soldiers, and God would reward both soldiers and supporters properly and generously.

ii. Jesus promised that even the help offered in a cup of cold water to one of His children would not be forgotten when God brings His reward (Matthew 10:42).

iii. This also explains why John would pray for the prosperity of Gaius: he used his resources in a godly way, being a blessing to others. If God blessed him with more, others would be blessed more also.

c. **Taking nothing from the Gentiles**: The ancient world of the early church was filled with the missionaries and preachers of various religions, and they often supported themselves by taking offerings from the general public. But John said that these Christian missionaries should take **nothing from the Gentiles** (non-Christians). Instead of soliciting funds from the general public they were to look to the support of fellow Christians.

d. **In a manner worthy of God**: Christians are not only called to help, but to help **in a manner worthy of God**. We are to do our best to help others excellently.

> i. Christians must first see that they are doing something to help the spread of the gospel. Then they must see that they do it **in a manner worthy of God**. God calls everyone of us to have a part in the great commission, the command of Matthew 28:19: *Go therefore and make disciples of all the nations, baptizing them in the name of the Father and of the Son and of the Holy Spirit.* One can have a part by going or have a part by helping, but everyone has a part and should do it well.

> ii. Jesus said, *He who receives you receives Me, and he who receives Me receives Him who sent Me. He who receives a prophet in the name of a prophet shall receive a prophet's reward. And he who receives a righteous man in the name of a righteous man shall receive a righteous man's reward* (Matthew 10:40-41). This should make us consider how we receive and help those who preach the Gospel.

2. (9-11) **Diotrephes**: A bad example.

**I wrote to the church, but Diotrephes, who loves to have the preeminence among them, does not receive us. Therefore, if I come, I will call to mind his deeds which he does, prating against us with malicious words. And not content with that, he himself does not receive the brethren, and forbids those who wish to, putting *them* out of the church. Beloved, do not imitate what is evil, but what is good. He who does good is of God, but he who does evil has not seen God.**

a. **But Diotrephes**: John publicly rebuked this man, and he rebuked him by name. In rebuking him by name the apostle of love did not act outside of love. Instead, he followed the clear command of the Scriptures (Romans 16:17) and the example of other apostles (2 Timothy 4:14-15).

> i. However, any such public rebuke must be made only when necessary, and we must be careful to not judge a brother against any standard that we ourselves would not be judged (Matthew 7:1-2).

> iii. By presenting himself as a "prominent Christian leader" (at least in his own mind), **Diotrephes** knew that he was open to public criticism - just as much as he would publicly criticize the apostle John and his associates (**prating against us with malicious words**).

b. **Who loves to have the preeminence among them**: Simply, the problem for **Diotrephes** was *pride*. In his pride, he did not **receive** the apostles such as John. This was in contrast to the humble hospitality of Gaius, who walked in the truth.

> i. We can imagine a man like Diotrephes, a leader in the church in some city, looking at John and saying to himself, "Why should these big shot apostles get all the attention and honor? Look at my ministry! Isn't it just as good?" And pride would lead him, like many others, to destruction.

> ii. Boice on **who loves to have the preeminence among them**: "This is the original and greatest of all sins. It is the sin of Satan, who was unwilling to be what God had created him to be and who desired rather to be 'like the Most High' (Isa. 14:14). It is the opposite of the nature of Christ 'who, being in very nature God, did not consider equality with God something to be grasped, but made himself nothing, taking the very nature of a servant.' "

c. **Prating against us with malicious words**: Diotrephes not only failed to receive John and the other apostles, but he also spoke against them. His malicious gossip against the apostles showed what kind of man he really was.

> i. "The Greek verb which is here translated 'gossiping' comes from a root which was used of the action of water in boiling up and throwing off bubbles. Since bubbles are empty and useless, the verb eventually came to mean indulgence in empty or useless talk. This was the nature of Diotrephes' slander, though, of course, the words were no less evil in that they were groundless." (Boice)

> ii. "The word signifieth . . . to talk big bubbles of words . . . it is a metaphor taken from over-seething pots, that send forth a foam; or . . . from overcharged stomachs, that must needs belch." (Trapp)

d. **Putting them out of the church**: Diotrephes not only used his influence to forbid others from showing hospitality to John or his associates; he even tried to excommunicate those who tried to show such hospitality.

> i. "To begin with, a man named Diotrephes had assumed an unwarranted and pernicious authority in the church, so much so that by the time of the writing of this letter John's own authority had been challenged and those who had been sympathetic to John had been excommunicated from the local assembly. Moreover, due to this struggle, traveling missionaries had been rudely treated, including probably an official delegation from John." (Boice)

> ii. The example of Diotrephes shows that those who love **to have the preeminence** also love to use whatever power they think they have as a sword against others.

e. **Do not imitate what is evil, but what is good**: John gave us two clear examples, one good (Gaius) and one bad (Diotrephes), and he now applies the point - follow the good, for we serve a good God and those who follow Him will likewise do good.

> i. John did not excommunicate Diotrephes, though as an apostle he had the authority to do so. Instead, he simply exposed him – and he trusted that discerning Christians would avoid Diotrephes as they should.

3. (12) **Demetrius**: A good example.

**Demetrius has a *good* testimony from all, and from the truth itself. And we also bear witness, and you know that our testimony is true.**

> a. **Demetrius has a good testimony from all**: John recommended this man to Gaius. Perhaps he was the one who carried the letter from John to Gaius, and John wanted Gaius to know that Demetrius was worthy of Christian hospitality.

> b. **Demetrius has a good testimony from all, and from the truth itself**: Demetrius was so faithful to the truth that even the truth was a witness on his behalf.

C. Conclusion.

1. (13-14a) John explains such a short letter to Gaius.

**I had many things to write, but I do not wish to write to you with pen and ink; but I hope to see you shortly, and we shall speak face to face.**

> a. **I had many things to write**: We can sympathize with John's preference for personal, face to face communication rather than the writing of letters. Yet we are thankful that John was forced to write, so that we have the record of this letter of 3 John.

2. (14b) Final blessings.

**Peace to you. Our friends greet you. Greet the friends by name.**

> a. **Our friends greet you**: In addition to a familiar blessing of **peace** upon Gaius, John also reminded him (and us) of the common ties of Christians - even if they are separated by miles, they are still **friends** in Jesus, and appropriately they should greet one another.

> b. **Peace to you**: This is a letter about contention and conflict; yet John appropriately ends the letter with a desire and expectation for **peace**. As Christians, we can and should have a sense of peace even in the midst of difficult times. Christians have the resources in Jesus Christ to have peace even in unsettled seasons.

# *Jude - Contending for the Faith*

*These shorter letters of the New Testament are often neglected, but the neglect of this important letter says more about us than it does about the Book of Jude. "Its neglect reflects more the superficiality of the generation that neglects it than the irrelevance of its burning message." (Guthrie)*

A. The danger that prompted Jude to write this letter.

1. (1) The author and the readers.

**Jude, a bondservant of Jesus Christ, and brother of James, To those who are called, sanctified by God the Father, and preserved in Jesus Christ:**

a. **Jude**: The name is literally "Judas." But to avoid connection with Judas Iscariot, the infamous man who betrayed Jesus, most English translators have used the name "**Jude**."

i. There are six people named "Judas" mentioned in the New Testament, but the best evidence identifies this as the one mentioned in Matthew 13:55 and Mark 6:3: **Jude**, the half-brother of Jesus.

ii. **Jude**, like the other half-brothers of Jesus (including James), didn't believe in Jesus as the Messiah until after the resurrection of Jesus (John 7:5 and Acts 1:14).

b. **A bondservant of Jesus Christ**: Jude was a *blood relative* of Jesus, but he considered himself only as **a bondservant of Jesus Christ**. The fact that he wanted himself to be known this way instead of introducing himself as "Jude, the half-brother of Jesus" tells us something of the humility of Jude and the relative unimportance of being connected to Jesus by human relationships.

i. Jesus spoke of this relative unimportance in passage such as Mark 3:31-35 and Luke 11:27-28.

ii. Without a doubt, Jude valued the fact that Jesus was his half-brother and that he grew up in the same household as Jesus. But even more valuable to him was his *new* relationship with Jesus. To Jude, the blood of the cross that saved him was more important than the family blood in his veins that related him to Jesus. Jude could say with Paul, *"Even though we have known Christ according to the flesh, yet now we know Him thus no longer"* (2 Corinthians 5:16).

c. **And brother of James**: James was an important leader of the church in Jerusalem and the author of the New Testament letter that bears his name. Both James and Jude were half-brothers of Jesus.

d. **To those who are called**: Jude wrote to Christians. This is not an evangelistic tract and it deals with things that believers need to hear, but often don't want to.

i. Jude identified his readers as Christians in three specific ways:

- They were **called**. A person is a Christian because God has **called** him. The important thing is to *answer* the call when it comes, just as we answer the telephone when it is ringing.

- They were **sanctified by God the Father**. This means that they were *set apart* - set apart from the world and set apart unto God.

- They were **preserved** in Jesus. Jesus Christ is our guardian and our protector.

2. (2) Jude gives a warm and typical greeting.

**Mercy, peace, and love be multiplied to you.**

a. **Mercy, peace, and love**: This is not the same greeting as found in most of Paul's letters (which usually begin with some variation of "Grace and peace unto you"). Yet it is substantially the same.

b. **Be multiplied to you**: In the mind and heart of Jude, it wasn't enough to have **mercy, peace, and love** *added* to the life of the Christian. He looked for *multiplication* instead of simple *addition*.

3. (3) The call to defend the faith.

**Beloved, while I was very diligent to write to you concerning our common salvation, I found it necessary to write to you exhorting you to contend earnestly for the faith which was once for all delivered to the saints.**

a. **I was very diligent to write to you**: Jude's initial desire was to write about our **common salvation**. But something happened - Jude **found it necessary to write** a different letter. We might say that this was the letter that didn't *want* to be written.

i. The letter of Jude is essentially a sermon. In it, Jude preached against the dangerous *practices* and *doctrines* that put the gospel of Jesus Christ in peril. These were serious issues and Jude dealt with them seriously.

ii. We should be happy that Jude was sensitive to the Holy Spirit here. What might have only been a letter from a Christian leader to a particular church instead became a precious instrument inspired by the Holy Spirit and valuable as a warning in these last days.

b. **Concerning our common salvation**: Our salvation isn't **common** in the sense that it is cheap or that everyone has it. It is **common** in the sense that we are saved in **common**, in community. God doesn't have one way for the rich and another way for the poor, or one way for the good and another way for the bad. We all come to God the same way. If it isn't a **common salvation**, it isn't *God's* salvation - and it isn't **salvation** at all.

i. An individual Christian may not know it, understand it, or benefit by it, but to be a Christian is to be a part of a community. To be a Christian means you stand shoulder to shoulder with millions of Christians who have gone before. We stand with strong Christians and weak Christians, brave Christians and cowardly Christians, old Christians and young Christians. We are part of an invisible, mighty army that spans back through the generations.

ii. "Upon other matters there are distinctions among believers, but yet there is a common salvation enjoyed by the Arminian as well as by the Calvinist, possessed by the Presbyterian as well as by the Episcopalian, prized by the Quaker as well as by the Baptist. Those who are in Christ are more near of kin than they know of, and their intense unity in deep essential truth is a greater force than most of them imagine: only give it scope and it will work wonders." (Spurgeon)

iii. In the 1980's a survey poll found that 70% of Americans who go to church say that you can be a *good* Christian without going to church. This doesn't match with Jude's idea of a **common salvation**.

c. **Exhorting you to contend earnestly for the faith**: This was the great need that Jude interrupted his intended letter to address. The ancient Greek word translated "**contend**" comes from the athletic world – from the wrestling mat. It is a *strengthened* form of the word meaning "to agonize." Therefore "**contend**" speaks of hard and diligent work.

i. The verb translated **contend earnestly** is (in the grammar of the ancient Greek) in the *present infinitive*, showing that the Christian struggle is continuous.

ii. We **contend earnestly for the faith** because it is valuable. If you walk into an art gallery and there are no guards or no sort of security system, you must draw one conclusion: there is nothing very valuable in that art gallery. Valuables are protected; worthless things are not.

d. **Exhorting you to contend earnestly for the faith**: If we emphasize the word **you**, we see that this was something that Jude wanted each individual Christian to do. There are many ways that every Christian can **contend earnestly for the faith.**

i. We contend for the faith in a *positive* sense when we give an unflinching witness, distribute tracts, make possible the training of faithful ambassadors for Jesus, or when we strengthen the hands of faithful pastors who honor the Word of God in their pulpits. These are a few among many ways that we can **contend earnestly for the faith** in a *positive* sense.

ii. We contend for the faith in a *negative* way when we withhold support and encouragement from false teachers.

iii. We contend for the faith in a *practical* sense when we live uncompromising Christian lives and give credit to the Lord who changed us.

iv. Obviously, faithful missionaries and evangelists **contend earnestly for the faith**. But so does the Sunday School teacher or the home group leaders, who is faithful to the Scriptures. People like this contend for the faith just as much as a front-line missionary does, and each one of us should contend for the gospel wherever God puts us.

e. **Contend earnestly for the faith once for all delivered to the saints**: Here, Jude tells us what we are contending *for*. There is a lot of earnest contention in the world but usually not for the right things. **The faith once for all delivered to the saints** is something *worth* contending for.

i. "**The faith**" doesn't mean our own personal belief, or **faith** in the sense of our trust in God. The phrase **the faith** means "The essential truths of the gospel that all true Christians hold in common." **The faith** is used in this sense repeatedly in the New Testament (Acts 6:7, 13:8, 14:22, 16:5, 24:24; Romans 1:5 and 16:26; Colossians 2:7, and 1 Timothy 1:2 are just some of the examples). We must **contend earnestly** for the *truth*. "*The faith* is the body of truth that very early in the church's history took on a definite form (cf. Acts 2:42; Romans 6:17; Galatians 1:23)." (Blum)

ii. **Once** means that the **faith** was **delivered** one time, and doesn't need to be **delivered** again. Of course, we *distribute* this truth again and again. But it was delivered by God to the world through the apostles and prophets **once** (Ephesians 2:20). God may speak today, but *never* in the authoritative way that He spoke through the first apostles and prophets as recorded in the New Testament. "There is no other gospel, there will be none. Its content will be more fully understood, its implications will be developed, its predictions will be fulfilled; but it will never be supplemented or succeeded or supplanted." (Erdman)

iii. **For all** means that this **faith** is for *everybody*. We don't have the option to simply make up our own faith and still be true to God. This faith is for **all**, but today, it isn't popular to really believe in **the faith once for all delivered to the saints**. Instead, most people want to believe in **the faith** they make up as they go along and decide is right for them. More people believe in "the faith that is in my heart" than **the faith once for all delivered to the saints**.

iv. In the book *Habits of the Heart*, Robert Bellah and his colleagues wrote about an interview with a young nurse named Sheila Larson, whom they described as representing many American's experience and views on religion. Speaking about her own faith and how it operated in her life, she said: "I believe in God. I'm not a religious fanatic. I can't remember the last time I went to church. My faith has carried me a long way. It is 'Sheilaism.' Just my own little voice." We might say that this highly individualistic faith is the most popular religion in the world, but the idea that we *can* or *should* put together our own faith is wrong. Christianity is based on one **faith**, which was **once for all delivered to the saints**.

4. (4) We need to contend for the faith because there are dangerous men among Christians.

**For certain men have crept in unnoticed, who long ago were marked out for this condemnation, ungodly men, who turn the grace of our God into lewdness and deny the only Lord God and our Lord Jesus Christ.**

a. **Certain men have crept in unnoticed**: In part, this is what makes them so dangerous – they are **unnoticed**. No one noticed that they were dangerous. They didn't wear a "Danger: False Teacher" name tag. These **certain men** probably claimed to be *more* Biblical than anybody else was.

i. **Crept in** means, "To slip in secretly as if by a side door." (Robertson) "Satan knows right well that one devil in the church can do far more than a thousand devils outside her bounds." (Spurgeon)

b. **Who long ago were marked out for this condemnation**: These **certain men** have a destiny - the destiny of every false teacher and leader. They are **marked** and destined **for this condemnation**, and it is enough to say that they are **ungodly men**. They are **ungodly** simply in the sense that they are not like God and no matter the outward appearances, they disregard God.

i. They were **unnoticed** by men, but not by God. The Lord is not wringing His hands in heaven, worrying about those who deceive others through their teaching and through their lifestyles. They may be hidden to some believers but as far as God is concerned, their **condemnation** was **marked out** long ago. Their judgment is assured. The truth will win out; our responsibility is to be on the side with the truth.

c. **Who turn the grace of our God into lewdness**: These **certain men** had received something of the **grace of God**. But when they received it, they turned it into an excuse for their **lewdness**.

i. The idea behind the ancient word **lewdness** is sin that is practiced without shame, without any sense of conscience or decency. Usually the word is used in the sense of sensual sins, such as sexual immorality. But it can also be used in the sense of brazen anti-biblical teaching, when the truth is denied and lies are taught without shame. Jude probably had both ideas in mind here, because as the rest of the letter will develop, these **certain men** had *both* moral problems and doctrinal problems.

ii. These words of Jude show that there is a *danger* in preaching grace. There are some who may take the truth of God's grace and **turn the grace of our God into lewdness**. But this doesn't mean there is anything wrong or dangerous about the message of God's grace. It simply shows how corrupt the human heart is.

d. **And deny the only Lord God and our Lord Jesus Christ**: These *certain men* **deny** the Lord Jesus Christ. They do this by refusing to recognize who Jesus said He was, and therefore they also deny who God the Father is also.

i. We are not told specifically how these men **deny the only Lord God**. It may be that they denied Him with their ungodly living or it may be that they denied Him with their heretical doctrines. Probably both were true.

B. Three examples that show the certainty of God's judgment against the *certain men*.

1. (5) The example of the people of Israel.

**But I want to remind you, though you once knew this, that the Lord, having saved the people out of the land of Egypt, afterward destroyed those who did not believe.**

a. **But I want to remind you, though you once knew this**: Jude knew he wasn't telling them anything new. They were already taught this example, but they needed to hear it again and to apply it to their present situation.

i. Ideally, every Christian would read these allusions to the Old Testament and say, "Yes Jude, I know *exactly* what you are talking about." If we don't know what Jude wrote about, it shows we need to deepen our understanding of the Bible.

ii. "As for the root facts, the fundamental doctrines, the primary truths of Scripture, we must from day to day insist upon them. We must never say of them, 'Everybody knows them'; for, alas! everybody forgets them." (Spurgeon)

iii. "The use of God's Word is not only to teach what we could not have otherwise known, but also to rouse us to a serious meditation of those things which we already understand, and not to suffer us to grow torpid in a cold knowledge." (Calvin)

b. **The Lord, having saved the people out of the land of Egypt**: Jude reminds us of what happened in Numbers 14. God delivered the people of Israel out of slavery in Egypt. They went out of Egypt and without unintended delays came to a place called Kadesh Barnea, on the threshold of the Promised Land. But at Kadesh Barnea, the people refused to trust God and go into the Promised Land of Canaan. Therefore almost none of the adult generation who left Egypt entered into the Promised Land.

i. Think of what God did for the people of Israel in this situation, and then how they responded to Him. They experienced God's miraculous deliverance at the Red Sea. They heard the very voice of God at Mount Sinai. They received His daily care and provision of manna in the wilderness. Yet they *still* lapsed into unbelief, and never entered into the place of blessing and rest God had for them.

c. **Afterward destroyed those who did not believe**: Those who doubted and rejected God at Kadesh Barnea paid a bigger price than just not entering the Promised Land. They also received the judgment of God. Psalm 95 describes how the Lord reacted to them: *For forty years I was grieved with that generation, and said, "It is a people who go astray in their hearts, and they do not know My ways. So I swore in My wrath, they shall not enter My rest"* (Psalm 95:10-11).

i. The warning through Jude is clear. The people of Israel started out from Egypt well enough. They had many blessings from God along the way. But they did not endure to the end, because they **did not believe** God's promise of power and protection.

ii. This example gives two lessons. First, it *assures* us that the *certain men* causing trouble will certainly be judged, even though they may have started out well in their walk with God. Jude says, "The certain men might have started out well. But so did the children of Israel, and God **afterward destroyed those who did not believe.**" Secondly, it warns us that *we also* must follow Jesus to the end, and never be among **those who did not believe**. The final test of our Christianity is *endurance*. Some start the race but never finish it.

2. (6) The example of the angels who sinned.

**And the angels who did not keep their proper domain, but left their own abode, He has reserved in everlasting chains under darkness for the judgment of the great day;**

a. **The angels who did not keep their proper domain**: Jude's letter is famous for bringing up obscure or controversial points, and this is one of them. Jude speaks of **the angels** who sinned, who are now imprisoned and awaiting a future day of judgment.

i. "It is not too much to say that the New Testament no where else presents so many strange phenomenon, or raises so many curious questions within so narrow a space." (Salmond, *Pulpit Commentary*)

b. **Angels who did not keep their proper domain**: There is some measure of controversy about the identity of these particular angels. We only have two places in the Bible where it speaks of angels sinning. First, there was the original rebellion of some angels against God (Isaiah 14:12-14, Revelation 12:4). Secondly, there was the sin of the *sons of God* described in Genesis 6:1-2.

i. Genesis 6:1-2 is a controversial passage all on its own. It says, *Now it came to pass, when men began to multiply on the face of the earth, and daughters were born to them, that the sons of God saw the daughters of men, that they were beautiful; and they took wives for themselves of all whom they chose.* There is a significant debate as to if the *sons of God* are angelic beings, or just another way of saying "followers of God" among humans. Jude helps us answer this question.

c. **Did not keep their proper domain, but left their own abode**: This offence was connected with some kind of *sexual* sin, such as the sexual union between rebellious angelic beings (the *sons of God* in Genesis 6:2) and the human beings (the *daughters of men* in Genesis 6:2). We know that there was some sexual aspect to this sin because Jude tells us in the following verse, Jude 7: *as Sodom and Gomorrah, and the cities around them in a similar manner to these, having given themselves over to sexual immorality and gone after strange flesh.* The words *in a similar manner to these* refers back to the **angels** of Jude 6, and the words *gone after strange flesh* refers to their unnatural sexual union.

i. We know some things about this unnatural sexual union from Genesis 6. We know that this unnatural union produced unnatural offspring. The unnatural union corrupted the genetic pool of mankind, so God had to find Noah, a man *perfect in his generations* (Genesis 6:9) - that is, "pure in his genetics." This unnatural union prompted an incredibly drastic judgment of God - a global flood, wiping out all of mankind except for eight people.

ii. We can add another piece of knowledge from Jude 6. This unnatural union prompted God to uniquely imprison the angels who sinned in this way. They are **reserved in everlasting chains under darkness for the judgment of the great day**.

iii. As for the *specific* details of this unnatural union, it is useless to speculate. We don't know how "fallen angel" genetic material could mix with human genetic material. Perhaps it happened through a unique form of demon possession and the fallen angel worked through a human host. We know that angels have the ability to assume human appearance at least temporarily, but we don't know more than that.

d. **He has reserved in everlasting chains under darkness for the judgment of the great day**: God judged these wicked angels, setting them in **everlasting chains**. Apparently some fallen angels are in bondage while others are unbound and active among mankind as demons.

i. By not keeping their **proper** place, they are now kept in **chains**. Their sinful pursuit of freedom put them in bondage. In the same way, those who insist on the freedom to do whatever they want are like these angels - bound with **everlasting chains**. True freedom comes from obedience.

ii. If angels cannot break the chains sin brought upon them, we are foolish to think that humans can break them. We can't set ourselves free from these chains, but we can only be set free by Jesus.

iii. This reminds us that these angels who sinned with an unnatural sexual union are no longer active. With His radical judgment back in the days of Noah, God put an end to this kind of unnatural sexual union.

iv. This example gives two lessons. First, it *assures* us that the *certain men* causing trouble will be judged, no matter what their spiritual status had been. These angels at one time stood in the immediate, glorious presence of God - and now they are in **everlasting chains**. If God judged the angels who sinned, He will judge these *certain men*. Secondly, it warns us that *we also* must continue walking with Jesus. If the past spiritual experience of these angels didn't guarantee their future spiritual state, then neither does ours. We must keep walking and be on guard.

3. (7) The example of Sodom and Gomorrah.

**As Sodom and Gomorrah, and the cities around them in a similar manner to these, having given themselves over to sexual immorality and gone after strange flesh, are set forth as an example, suffering the vengeance of eternal fire.**

a. **As Sodom and Gomorrah**: These two cities (**and the cities around them**) also stand as examples of God's judgment. Their sin - which was most conspicuously homosexuality, but included other sins as well - brought forth God's judgment.

i. Sodom and Gomorrah were blessed, privileged places. They were situated in a blessed area: it was *well watered everywhere . . . like the garden of the LORD* (Genesis 13:10).

b. **Having given themselves over to sexual immorality and gone after strange flesh**: Jude refers to the account in Genesis 19, where the homosexual conduct of the men of Sodom is described. Ezekiel 16:49 tells us of other sins of Sodom: *Look, this was the iniquity of your sister Sodom: She and her daughter had pride, fullness of food, and abundance of idleness; neither did she strengthen the hand of the poor and needy.* Sexual depravity was not their *only* sin, but it was certainly *among* their sins, and Jude makes this plain.

i. The sins described in Ezekiel 16:49 show that Sodom and Gomorrah were indeed prosperous, blessed areas. You don't have *fullness of food, and abundance of idleness* if you don't have material blessings. But despite their great blessing from God and material prosperity, they sinned and were judged.

c. **Suffering the vengeance of eternal fire**: In Genesis 19, Sodom and Gomorrah were destroyed with fire from heaven. But that wasn't the end of their judgment by fire. Far worse than what happened in Genesis 19, they suffered **the vengeance of eternal fire**.

i. This example gives two lessons. First, it *assures* us that the *certain men* causing trouble will be judged, no matter how much they had been blessed in the past. Just as Sodom and Gomorrah were once wonderfully blessed but eventually suffered **the vengeance of eternal fire**, so will it be with these *certain men*. Secondly, it warns us that *we also* must continue walking with Jesus. If the blessings of the past didn't guarantee their future spiritual state, then neither does ours.

C. More sins of the *certain men*.

1. (8) The character of these dangerous *certain men*.

**Likewise also these dreamers defile the flesh, reject authority, and speak evil of dignitaries.**

a. **Likewise also**: Jude connected the *certain men* with the people of Sodom and Gomorrah in their *sensuality* (**defile the flesh**) and in their rejection of God's authority (**reject authority**).

> i. When Jude pointed out that these *certain men* **reject authority**, it meant that *they* wanted to be in authority. Therefore they rejected the authority of God and they rejected those God put in authority.

> ii. Today, our culture encourages us to **reject authority** and to recognize *self* as the only real authority in our lives. We can do this with the Bible, by choosing to only believe certain passages. We can do it with our beliefs, by choosing at the "salad bar" of religion. Or we can do it with our lifestyle, by making our own rules and not recognizing the proper authorities God has established.

> iii. In the darkest days of Israel, society was characterized by a term: *every man did what was right in his own eyes* (Judges 21:25). Today, this is the pattern of all the world and especially Western civilization.

b. **These dreamers**: It is possible that Jude meant that the *certain men* were out of touch with reality. It is more likely that he meant they claimed to have prophetic dreams which were really deceptions.

c. **Speak evil of dignitaries**: Probably these **dignitaries** were the apostles or other leaders in the church. Their rejection of **authority** was connected with their speaking **evil of dignitaries**.

2. (9) Michael the archangel as an example of someone who would not speak evil of dignitaries.

**Yet Michael the archangel, in contending with the devil, when he disputed about the body of Moses, dared not bring against him a reviling accusation, but said, "The Lord rebuke you!"**

a. **Michael the archangel . . . the devil**: Jude mentioned two kinds of angelic beings. **Michael** is among the angelic beings faithful to God, who are the servants of God and man. **The devil** is among the angelic beings rebelling against God, who are the enemies of man.

> i. There are invisible, angelic beings all around us. There are ministering spirits sent by God to assist us, and demonic spirits who want to defeat us. The devil can't unsave a saved person; but through his deceptions he can corrupt and defile a Christian who is supposed to walk in purity and freedom. To the devil, we are time bombs, ready to wreck his work — bombs that he would like to defuse and make ineffective.

> ii. Many people today don't believe **the devil** exists, but the Bible says he does. Or, if they believe he exists, they think of him in funny images from the Middle Ages. Back then, *miracle plays* were a chief form

of entertainment. They were sort of a pageant where religious stories were acted out on stage. The audience learned to look for one character that was always dressed in red, wore horns on his head, and had a tail dangling behind him. His shoes looked like cloven hoofs, and he had a pitchfork in his hand. The audience was amused by this silly characterization of Satan, and got the idea that he was sort of a comical character. The devil doesn't mind being thought of this way.

b. **Michael the archangel**: This angelic being is mentioned by name in four passages of the Bible: Daniel 10, Daniel 12, Revelation 12 and here in Jude. Every time **Michael** appears, it is in the context of battle or readiness to fight. He is an **archangel**, which simply means a "leading angel."

i. If **the devil** has an opposite, it certainly isn't God. It is **Michael the archangel** – another high ranking angelic being.

ii. "Let it be observed that the word *archangel* is never found in the *plural* number in the sacred writings. There can be properly only one *archangel*, one chief or head of all the angelic host. Nor is the word *devil*, as applied to the great enemy of mankind, ever found in the plural; there can be but one monarch of all fallen spirits." (Clarke)

c. **When he disputed about the body of Moses**: This is another obscure reference by Jude. The last we read about **the body of Moses** is in Deuteronomy 34:5-6: *So Moses, the servant of the LORD died there in the land of Moab, according to the word of the LORD. And He buried him in a valley in the land of Moab, opposite Beth Peor; but no one knows the grave to this day.*

i. We don't know where Jude received his information about this dispute. He may have received a unique revelation from God. But according to teachers in the early church, Jude referred to an apocryphal book known as the *Assumption of Moses*, of which only small portions survive.

ii. We don't even exactly know why there was a dispute **about the body of Moses**. Some have said that the devil wanted to use Moses' body as an object of worship to lead Israel astray into idolatry. Others have thought that Satan wanted to desecrate the body of Moses, and claimed a right to it because Moses had murdered an Egyptian.

iii. It is more likely that the devil anticipated a purpose God had for Moses' body, and the devil tried to defeat that plan. We know that after his death, Moses appeared in bodily form at the Transfiguration (Matthew 17:1-3) with Elijah (whose body was caught up to heaven in 2 Kings 2). Perhaps also Moses and Elijah are the two witnesses of Revelation 11, and God needed Moses' body for that future plan.

iv. But for Jude, the main point isn't *why* Michael was disputed, but *how* he disputed with the devil.

d. **Dared not bring against him a reviling accusation, but said, "The Lord rebuke you!"** The manner of Michael's fight is a model for spiritual warfare. First, we see that Michael was *in a battle*. Secondly, we see that he battled in the *Lord's authority*.

i. This proves to us that Michael is *not* Jesus, as some heretical groups have thought. Jesus rebuked the devil in *His own* authority, but Michael did not. "The point of contrast is that Michael could not reject the devil's accusation on his own authority." (Bauckham)

ii. Significantly, Michael **dared not bring against him a reviling accusation**. Michael did not mock or accuse the devil. God hasn't called us to judge the devil, to condemn the devil, to mock him or accuse him, but to battle against him in the name of the Lord.

iii. This relates to the *certain men* by a "how much more" line of thinking. If Michael **dared not bring against him a reviling accusation** against *the devil*, how much more should these *certain men* not speak evil of dignitaries.

3. (10) More of the bad character of the *certain men*.

**But these speak evil of whatever they do not know; and whatever they know naturally, like brute beasts, in these things they corrupt themselves.**

a. **But these speak evil**: In contrast to Michael, who would not even speak evil of the devil, these *certain men* spoke evil, especially when they rejected authority and spoke against dignitaries.

b. **Of whatever they do not know**: The *certain men* didn't even know the things or the people they spoke evil about. Their evil speech was made worse by their ignorance.

i. Since they also spoke against dignitaries and rejected authority, these *certain men* did **not know** about true spiritual leadership and authority - so they found it easy to **speak evil** against it.

c. **Whatever they know naturally, like brute beasts, in these things they corrupt themselves**: These *certain men* pretended to be spiritual, but their only knowledge was really *natural*. Even what they knew **naturally**, they still used to corrupt themselves with an unspiritual mind.

i. **Brute beasts** can be smart or clever in an instinctive way, but they obviously do not have spiritual knowledge. It was the same way with these *certain men*.

ii. "How ironical that when men should claim to be knowledgeable, they should actually be ignorant; when they think themselves superior to the common man they should actually be on the same level as animals, and be corrupted by the very practices in which they seek liberty and self-expression." (Green)

D. Three examples of the *certain men*.

1. (11a) The *certain men* have gone in the way of Cain.

**Woe to them! For they have gone in the way of Cain,**

a. **The way of Cain**: Cain's story is found in Genesis 4. Each of the sons of Adam and Eve brought an offering to the Lord. Cain (being a farmer) brought an offering from his harvest. Abel (being a shepherd) brought an offering from his flocks. God accepted Abel's offering, but He rejected Cain's sacrifice.

i. Many people assume that because Abel brought a blood sacrifice and Cain brought a grain sacrifice, that the difference between the two offerings was sacrificial blood. But the real difference was between *faith* and *unbelief.* Hebrews 11:4 makes this plain: *By faith Abel offered to God a more excellent sacrifice than Cain, through which he obtained witness that he was righteous, God testifying of his gifts; and through it he being dead still speaks.*

ii. Cain's sacrifice was probably more pleasing to the senses than the carcass of a dead lamb. But his sacrifice was offered without faith, and therefore it was unacceptable to God. You can give to God whatever you have or whatever you are, but you must offer it *in faith.*

b. **The way of Cain**: Genesis 4:5 says that after God rejected his sacrifice, *Cain was very angry, and his countenance fell.* He became angry because he knew he was rejected by God. In a fit of anger Cain murdered Abel, and then he lied about it to God.

i. 1 John 3:12 tells us that Cain murdered his brother because Abel's works were righteous (by faith), while Cain's own were wicked. Cain's lack was not in works, but in faith.

c. **The way of Cain**: Jude says that Cain typifies a **way** that the *certain men* follow in. It is **the way of** unbelief and empty religion, which leads to jealousy, persecution of the truly godly, and eventually to murderous anger.

i. There is no greater curse on the earth than empty, vain religion; those who have *a form of godliness but denying its power* (2 Timothy 3:5). No wonder Paul added, *and from such people turn away!*

ii. Many Christians are afraid of secular humanism or atheism or the world. But dead religion is far more dangerous, and sends more people to hell than anything else. These *certain men* were **in the way of Cain**, which is the way of dead religion.

2. (11b) The *certain men* are in the error of Balaam.

## Have run greedily in the error of Balaam for profit,

a. **The error of Balaam**: Balaam's story is in Numbers 22 to 25 and 31. During the time of the Exodus, Israel advanced to the land of Moab, after defeating the Amorites. When the Israelites came near, King Balak of Moab sought the help of a prophet named Balaam.

i. The first delegation from King Balak arrived and God told Balaam to have nothing to do with them. God's initial words to Balaam were, *"You shall not go with them; you shall not curse the people, for they are blessed"* (Numbers 22:12).

ii. After the first visit another, more prestigious delegation came with great riches. Balaam wanted to go with them and God allowed him to go. Balaam lusted after the riches and prestige offered to him and God gave him over to his own sin.

iii. God warned Balaam to turn back when he was on the way to see Balak. Yet his heart was set on the rich reward King Balak promised and he continued on. Balaam even ignored a talking donkey, sent to warn him to turn back.

iv. Balaam knew that he has done wrong. In Numbers 22:34, he said to God *I have sinned . . . Now therefore, if it displeases You, I will turn back*. But he didn't turn back. He continued on, refusing to see that when God says no, we must take it as a no. Instead, God gave Balaam what his sinful heart desired.

v. After meeting with King Balak of Moab, Balaam prophesied over Israel four times. But as he spoke forth God's word, he did not curse Israel – instead he blessed her each time. When he was unsuccessful in cursing Israel, Balaam advised Balak on how to bring Israel under a curse. Instead of trying to have a prophet curse Israel, he should lead her into fornication and idolatry and then God would curse a disobedient Israel.

vi. Balak did just that, sending his young women into the camp of Israel to lead Israel into sexual immorality and idolatry. Because of the people's sin, God did curse Israel - He brought a plague of judgment upon Israel that killed 24,000. Therefore Balaam was guilty of the greatest of sins: deliberately leading others into sin. Worse yet, he did it for money.

b. **Greedily in the error of Balaam for profit**: The greedy **error of Balaam** was that he was willing to compromise everything for money. The *certain men* Jude warned about had the same heart.

i. Many Christians would never deny Jesus under persecution, but might deny Him if offered a large sum of money. There is not a single sin that corrupt man will not commit for the sake of money. Covetousness is such a dangerous sin that it killed Jesus - 30 pieces of silver helped put Jesus on the cross.

ii. **Have run greedily** is literally "they were poured out" (Robertson). This is a strong picture of excessive indulgence. But Paul also uses the same term for the extravagant way God loves us: *the love of God has been poured out in our hearts* (Romans 5:5).

3. (11c) The *certain men* live out the rebellion of Korah.

**And perished in the rebellion of Korah.**

a. **The rebellion of Korah**: Korah's story is found in Numbers 16. He was a prominent man in Israel, and one day came to Moses, saying, *You take too much upon yourself, for all the congregation is holy, every one of them, and the LORD is among them. Why then do you exalt yourself about the congregation of the LORD?* (Numbers 16:3) Korah and his followers resented the authority God gave to Moses and Aaron.

i. When Korah said this, Moses fell on his face, knowing God's judgment would soon come. Moses then proposed a test: each group took censers (for burning incense) and came before the Lord. The Lord Himself would choose which man He wanted to represent Him: Moses or Korah.

ii. When they both came before God, the Lord told Moses to step away. Then, the ground opened up and swallowed Korah and his followers. After that, fire came down from heaven and burned up all of his supporters. They all **perished**.

b. **Rebellion**: Korah was a Levite, but not of the priestly family of Aaron. As a Levite, he had had his own God-appointed sphere of ministry, yet he was not content with it. He wanted the ministry and the authority of Moses.

i. Korah needed to learn this essential lesson: we should work hard to fulfill everything God has called us to be. At the same time, we should never try to be what God has *not* called us to be.

c. **The rebellion of Korah**: This was also a rejection of God's appointed leaders, especially God's appointed Mediator. When the *certain men* rejected authority and spoke evil against dignitaries, they walked in **the rebellion of Korah**.

i. The rebellion of Korah "lies in the broader idea of a contemptuous and determined assertion of self against divinely appointed ordinances." (Salmond, *The Pulpit Commentary*)

ii. These three men came from quite different backgrounds: Cain was a farmer, Balaam was a prophet, and Korah was a leader in Israel. Apostasy is never confined to one group of people. "There are apostates in the pulpit, in the palace, and in the poorhouse." (Coder)

E. What the future holds for these *certain men.*

1. (12-13) A vivid description of the depravity of these *certain men.*

**These are spots in your love feasts, while they feast with you without fear, serving *only* themselves. *They are* clouds without water, carried about by the winds; late autumn trees without fruit, twice dead, pulled up by the roots; raging waves of the sea, foaming up their own shame; wandering stars for whom is reserved the blackness of darkness forever.**

a. **Spots in your love feasts**: The early Christians often met for a common meal, something like a potluck dinner. They called these meals **love feasts**, or "Agape Feasts." When these *certain men* came, they were **serving only themselves**. They ate greedily at the **love feasts** while others went hungry.

i. At the Agape Feast, everybody brought what they could - some a little, some a lot; but they all shared it together. For some slaves who were Christians it might have been the only decent meal they regularly ate. The selfishness of these *certain men* spoiled the fellowship. 1 Corinthians 11:17-34 describes a similar problem in the Corinthian church.

ii. It always spoils fellowship when we come to church with a selfish "bless me" attitude. Many who would never eat selfishly at a church meal still come to church concerned with **serving only themselves**.

iii. **Spots**: Some Greek scholars think this word should be translated "hidden rocks" instead of **spots**. One way or another, it doesn't make much real difference to the meaning of the passage.

iv. **Serving only themselves**: Literally in the ancient Greek this is "shepherding themselves" (Robertson). They were shepherds of a sort - but only shepherding **themselves**.

b. **Clouds without water, carried by the winds**: **Clouds** without water are good for nothing. They bring no life-giving rain and they only block out the sun. They exist just for themselves. The *certain men* were like these **clouds**.

i. Once while driving by a factory, my daughter Aan-Sofie looked at the billows of white smoke coming from the smoke stacks. She said, "That's where they make clouds!" These *certain men* were like those empty clouds – good for nothing, **carried by the winds**, floating on the breeze from one fad to another.

c. **Late autumn trees without fruit**: By **late autumn**, trees should have **fruit**. But these *certain men* did not bear **fruit** even when they should. They were like trees that only take instead of give.

d. **Raging waves of the sea**: For modern man, the sea is often a thing of beauty. But to ancient man, especially in Biblical cultures, the sea was an unmanageable terror. Isaiah 57:20 expresses this idea: *But the wicked are like the troubled sea, when it cannot rest, whose waters cast up mire and dirt.* These *certain men* were busy and active like the **raging waves of the sea**, but all it brought was **foaming up their own shame.**

i. Busyness is no mark of correctness. The fruit of these men was like the foam or scum at the seashore. Jude has in mind the ugly shoreline after a storm has washed up all sorts of driftwood, seaweed and debris.

e. **Wandering stars**: Like comets streaking through the sky, these *certain men* astonished the world for a time, and then vanished into darkness. An unpredictable star was no good for guidance and navigation. Even so these deceivers were useless and untrustworthy.

f. **Blackness of darkness forever**: This described their destiny. Unless they repent, they would end up in hell - and be there **forever**.

i. The punishment of hell is **forever** because a *mere man* is paying for his own sins, offering an imperfect sacrifice which must be repeated over and over again for eternity. A perfect man can offer a single sacrifice; but an imperfect man must continually offer a sacrifice.

ii. Our obligations to God are infinite and can therefore only be satisfied in Jesus, an infinite person

2. (14-15) The certainty of judgment upon these *certain men*.

**Now Enoch, the seventh from Adam, prophesied about these men also, saying, "Behold, the Lord comes with ten thousands of His saints, to execute judgment on all, to convict all who are ungodly among them of all their ungodly deeds which they have committed in an ungodly way, and of all the harsh things which ungodly sinners have spoken against Him."**

a. **Now Enoch**: Here Jude quoted from Enoch, who is described in Genesis 5 and mentioned in Hebrews 11. The ancient book of Enoch was not received as Scripture, but it was highly respected among both the Jews and early Christians.

i. "Tertullian tells us that the book of Enoch's prophecies were preserved by Noah in the ark, and that they continued and were read until the times of the apostles. But because they contained many famous testimonies concerning Jesus Christ, the Jews out of malice suppressed and abolished the whole book." (Trapp)

ii. Jude did not quote from Enoch to tell us anything new, but to give a vivid description of what the Bible already teaches. The Apostle Paul also quoted non-Biblical sources on at least three different occasions (Acts 17:28, 1 Corinthians 15:33 and Titus 1:12). This wasn't to proclaim a new truth, but to support an already established Biblical principle.

iii. Jude's quoting of the book of Enoch doesn't mean that the whole book of Enoch inspired Scripture - only the portion Jude quotes. In the same way, when Paul quoted a pagan poet, he didn't mean that the entire work of the poet was inspired by God.

b. **To convict all who are ungodly**: In this quotation from the book of Enoch Jude emphasized the words **all** and **ungodly**. God is coming to judge **all** of the **ungodly**.

c. **To execute judgment on all**: Many people take the **judgment** of God lightly. But the most important question in the world is "Will God judge me? Am I accountable to Him?" If we are truly accountable to God, we are fools if we do not prepare to face that **judgment**.

i. Think of someone arrested for a crime, with a date to appear in court - but made absolutely no preparation for his appearance before the judge. That person would be a fool. We shouldn't be so foolish, and instead take advantage of our court-appointed advocate – Jesus Christ (1 John 2:1).

3. (16-18) The methods of the *certain men*.

**These are grumblers, complainers, walking according to their own lusts; and they mouth great swelling *words*, flattering people to gain advantage. But you, beloved, remember the words which were spoken before by the apostles of our Lord Jesus Christ: how they told you that there would be mockers in the last time who would walk according to their own ungodly lusts.**

a. **Grumblers, complainers . . . they mouth great swelling words, flattering people**: Jude noticed that their methods all revolved around **words**. On top of their questionable lives, they were essentially a people of deception, departing from the foundation of Jesus Christ, and the apostles and prophets.

b. **These are grumblers, complainers**: These people were **complainers**. It has rightly been observed that whenever a man gets out of touch with God, he is likely to begin complaining about something.

> i. Grumbling "is to insult the God who gives us all things; it is to forget that whatever befalls us, nothing can separate us from His love, nor deprive us of that most priceless of all treasures, the Lord's presence in our lives." (Green)

> ii. "You know the sort of people alluded to here, nothing ever satisfies them. They are discontented even with the gospel. The bread of heaven must be cut into three pieces, and served on dainty napkins, or else they cannot eat it; and very soon their soul hates even this light bread. There is no way by which a Christian man can serve God so as to please them. They will pick holes in every preacher's coat; and if the great High Priest himself were here, they would find fault with the color of the stones of his breastplate." (Spurgeon)

c. **Flattering people**: These *certain men* knew how to use smooth, flattering words to get an advantage over other people. They would say anything - good or bad - to get an advantage.

d. **But you, beloved, remember**: We are to be different. We are to remember what Jesus and the apostles said, **which were spoken by the apostles of our Lord Jesus Christ**. The word of God is always the answer to dangers in or out of the church.

> i. The apostles had warned that just these things would happen; and even more so as the day approaches: *For the time will come when they will not endure sound doctrine, but according to their own desires, because they have itching ears, they will heap up for themselves teachers; and they will turn their ears away from the truth, and be turned aside to fables* (2 Timothy 4:3-4).

e. **There would be mockers in the last time**: Perhaps Jude had in mind those who mock the idea of Jesus' return. Or he may mean the kind of men who mock those who don't go along the same path of destruction they travel on.

> i. **Mockers . . . who would walk according to their own ungodly lusts**: Those who live **according to their own ungodly lusts** love to mock those who want to please God. Jude wants Christians to *expect* this kind of mocking, so they won't be surprised by it.

4. (19) The spiritual status of these *certain men*.

**These are sensual persons, who cause divisions, not having the Spirit.**

a. **These are sensual persons**: Essentially, these men were not *spiritual*; they were carnal and insensitive to the Holy Spirit.

i. **Sensual** in this context has nothing to do with sexual attractiveness. It describes the person who lives only *by* and *for* what he can get through his physical senses, and he lives this way selfishly. His motto is, "If it feels good, do it" or, "How can it be wrong if it *feels* so right?"

b. **Who cause divisions**: These *certain men* had an instinct to separate themselves and make **divisions**. "The word, found only once in the Bible, denotes those superior people who keep themselves to themselves - Christian Pharisees." (Green)

c. **Not having the Spirit**: This same description could be written over many churches, or church projects, or evangelism campaigns, or home groups, or even individual Christian lives. The church and the world truly need genuinely *spiritual* men and women today.

F. What to do about the danger of the *certain men.*

*Significantly, Jude does not tell us to attack the certain men who are a danger to the church. Instead, he tells us to focus on our walk with the Lord, help others affected by the certain men, and to focus on God. We simply are to pay the certain men no attention, except for what is necessary for our warning. God will take care of them.*

1. (20-21) Take a look *inward.*

**But you, beloved, building yourselves up on your most holy faith, praying in the Holy Spirit, keep yourselves in the love of God, looking for the mercy of our Lord Jesus Christ unto eternal life.**

a. **Keep yourselves in the love of God**: We know that God loves even the ungodly (Romans 5:6). Therefore Jude doesn't mean, "Live in such a way to make yourself lovable to God." Instead, to **keep yourselves in the love of God** means to keep yourself in harmony with God's ever-present love.

i. But we should understand what it means when the Bible says that God loves the ungodly. The significance of the idea that God loves us all has been twisted considerably. Consider the sinner who defends his sinful practice by saying "God loves me just the way I am." His implication is that "God loves me; I must be pretty good." Actually, the fact that God loves him is a reflection on *God's* goodness, not his own. The perspective isn't, "I'm so great that *even* God loves me," but "God is so great that He loves *even* me."

ii. God's love extends everywhere, and nothing can separate us from it. But we can deny ourselves the benefits of God's love. People who don't **keep** themselves **in the love of God** end up living as if they are on the dark side of the moon. The sun is always out there, always shining, but they are never in a position to receive its light or warmth.

An example of this is the Prodigal Son of Luke 15, who was always loved by the father, but for a time he did not benefit from it.

b. **Building yourselves up on your most holy faith**: This is one way that we can keep ourselves in the love of God. It means to keep growing spiritually, and to keep building up. Jude tells us, "**build *yourselves* up on your most holy faith**." This means that we are responsible for our own spiritual growth. It means that we cannot wait for spiritual growth to just happen, or expect others to make us grow.

> i. Jude has shown us the frailty of men and how deceivers even infiltrated the church. If you entrust your spiritual growth to someone else, it will not only hurt your spiritual growth, but it may also lead you astray.

> ii. Others can help provide an environment conducive for spiritual growth. But no one can *make* another person grow in his relationship with the Lord.

> iii. **On your most holy faith**: The **most holy faith** is the same as *the faith once for all delivered to the saints* (Jude 3). Jude wasn't talking about growing *in* **the most holy faith** (though that is a valid idea). Jude is talking about growing **on your most holy faith**. We grow *on the foundation of the truth*.

c. **Praying in the Holy Spirit**: This is another way to keep ourselves in the love of God. The battle against wrong living and wrong teaching is a spiritual battle, requiring prayer in the Holy Spirit.

> i. Many of our prayers are directed by our own needs, by our own intellects, or by our own wishes and desires. But there is a higher level of prayer: *Likewise the Spirit also helps in our weaknesses. For we do not know what we should pray for as we ought, but the Spirit Himself makes intercession for us* (Romans 8:26).

> ii. The Holy Spirit may help us pray by giving us the right words to say when we pray. He may speak through *groanings which cannot be uttered* (Romans 8:26). Or the Holy Spirit may do it through the gift of tongues, a gift God gives to seeking hearts, which want to communicate with Him on a deeper level than normal conversation.

> iii. "Such is our sloth, and that such is the coldness of our flesh, that no one can pray aright except he be roused by the Spirit of God . . . no one can pray as he ought without having the Spirit as his guide." (Calvin)

d. **Looking for the mercy of Lord Jesus Christ unto eternal life**: This is a third way that we can keep ourselves in the love of God. As we keep the blessed hope of Jesus' soon return alive in our hearts, this effectively keeps us in the love of God, and helps us to *not* give away our faith.

2. (22-23) Take a look *outward*, to those around you.

**And on some have compassion, making a distinction; but others save with fear, pulling *them* out of the fire, hating even the garment defiled by the flesh.**

a. **On some have compassion**: Jude begins here to tell us what we must do with those who have been influenced by these *certain men*. We need to make **a distinction**, based on where they are coming from. Certainly, **on some have compassion**.

i. Using wisdom we approach different people in different manners. By being sensitive to the Holy Spirit, we can know when we should comfort, and when we should rebuke. Christians should not abandon a friend flirting with false teaching. They should help him through it in love.

ii. The means we continue to love them. No matter how bad a person is, or how misleading and terrible their doctrine, we are not allowed to hate them - or to be unconcerned for their salvation.

iii. **Compassion** often means watching over someone, helping them with accountability. "Meantime watch over others as well as yourselves; and give them such help as their various needs require." (Wesley)

b. **Others save with fear**: This second group must be confronted more strongly - but in **fear**, not in a sanctimonious superiority. You may need to pull **them out of the fire**, but never do it in pride.

i. This *outward* look is important. It demonstrates that we are not only concerned for our own spiritual welfare. It proves that we genuinely care about other Christians who are edging towards significant error.

3. (24-25) Take a look upward to the God of all glory

**Now to Him who is able to keep you from stumbling,**
**And to present *you* faultless**
**Before the presence of His glory with exceeding joy,**
**To God our Savior,**
**Who alone is wise,**
***Be* glory and majesty,**
**Dominion and power,**
**Both now and forever.**
**Amen.**

a. **Now to Him**: Jude closes the letter with a famous *doxology* (a brief declaration of praise to God). Jude's doxology reminds us of God's care and of our destiny.

b. **Who is able to keep you from stumbling, and to present you fault-less**: Jude's message of warning and doom might have depressed and discouraged his readers. Perhaps his original readers thought that with so much false teaching and immorality around, very few Christians would ever reach heaven. Here he reminds them that the answer lies only in the power of God. He **is able to keep you**, and you aren't able to keep yourself.

i. In mountain climbing, the beginning hiker attaches himself to the expert so that if he loses his footing he won't stumble and fall to his death. In the same manner, if we keep connected with God, we cannot fall. He keeps us safe.

ii. By comparing passages of Scripture, we also find out who is really responsible for our safe keeping. Jude began the letter by addressing those who are *preserved in Jesus* (Jude 1). Then he exhorted Christians to avoid dangerous men and to keep themselves *in the love of God* (Jude 21) Here at the end he concluded with the recognition that it is ultimately God who keeps us from stumbling and falling. Paul put the same idea in Philippians 2:12-13: *work out your own salvation with fear and trembling; for it is God who works in you both to will and to do for His good pleasure.*

iii. Keeping us spiritually safe *is* God's work. But you can always tell the people He is working in, because *they* are working also. God doesn't call us to simply let the Christian life happen to us and He doesn't command us to save ourselves. He calls us to a partnership with Him.

c. **Before the presence of His glory with exceeding joy**: As God is faithful, we won't have to slink shamefacedly into the presence of God. We can be presented before Him with **exceeding joy**.

d. **Who alone is wise, be glory and majesty, dominion and power, both now and forever**: This all reminds us of God's wisdom, glory, and power. Jude isn't trying to say that we can or should *give* these things to God. When we acknowledge and declare the truth about God, it glorifies Him. We aren't giving God more **majesty** or **power** than He had before; we are just recognizing and declaring it.

i. **Both now and forever**: This could also be translated "unto all the ages." This is "as complete a statement of eternity as can be made in human language." (Robertson) Our victory, our triumph in God, is **forever**.

ii. There is serious deception in the world and often among those called Christians. There are enemies of the gospel who have infiltrated the church. Yet despite the greatness of the threat, *God is greater still.* He wins, and if we will only stay with Him, we are guaranteed victory also.

iii. Jude is a book full of warning, but it closes with supreme confidence in God. Dangerous times should make us trust in a mighty God.

# The Books of 1-2-3 John and Jude
## Selected Bibliography

This is a bibliography of books cited in the commentary. Of course, there are many other worthy books on 1,2,3 John and Jude, but these are listed for the benefit of readers who wish to check sources.

Alford, Henry  *The New Testament for English Readers, Volume II, Part II* (London: Rivingtons, 1866)

Barclay, William  *The Letters of John and Jude* (Philadelphia: Westminster, 1976)

Barker, Glenn W.  "1,2,3 John" *Expositor's Bible Commentary, Volume 12* (Grand Rapids: Zondervan, 1981)

Barnes, Albert  *Notes on the New Testament, James, Peter, John and Jude* (Grand Rapids: Baker, 1975)

Bauckham, Richard J.  *Jude, 2 Peter* (Waco: Word Books, 1983)

Blum, Edwin A.  "Jude" *Expositor's Bible Commentary, Volume 12* (Grand Rapids: Zondervan, 1981)

Boice, James Montgomery  *The Epistles of John, An Expositional Commentary* (Grand Rapids: Zondervan, 1979)

Calvin, John  "Commentaries on the Epistle of Jude" *Calvin's Commentaries Volume XXII* (Grand Rapids: Baker, 1979)

Clarke, Adam  *The New Testament of Our Lord and Saviour Jesus Christ, Volume II* (New York: Eaton & Mains, 1832)

Coder, S. Maxwell  *Jude: The Acts of the Apostates* (Chicago: Moody Press, 1986)

Erdman, Charles  *The General Epistles* (Philadelphia: Westminster, 1966)

Friederichsen, Mrs. Paul  *God's Truth Made Simple – Studies from First John* (Chicago: Moody Bible Institute, 1966)

Green, Michael  _The Second Epistle of Peter and the Epistle of Jude_ (Grand Rapids: Eerdmans, 1982)

Guthrie, Donald  _New Testament Introduction_ (Downer's Grove, Illinois: InterVarsity/Tyndale, 1970)

Lenski, R.C.H.  _The Interpretation of The Epistle to the Hebrews and The Epistle of James_ (Minneapolis, Minnesota: Augsburg Publishing House, 1966)

Lewis, C.S.  _The Four Loves_ (New York: Harcourt Brace Jovanovich, 1960)

Maclaren, Alexander  _Expositions of Holy Scripture, Volume 17_ (Grand Rapids: Baker, 1984)

Manton, Thomas  _Commentary of Jude_ (Grand Rapids: Kregel, 1988 reprint of 1658 edition)

Marshall, I. Howard  _The Epistles of John_ (Grand Rapids: Eerdmans, 1978)

Meyer, F.B.  _Our Daily Homily_ (Westwood, New Jersey: Revell, 1966)

Morgan, G. Campbell  _An Exposition of the Whole Bible_ (Old Tappan, New Jersey: Revell, 1959)

Morgan, G. Campbell  _Searchlights from the Word_ (New York: Revell, 1926)

Poole, Matthew  _A Commentary on the Holy Bible, Volume III: Matthew-Revelation_ (London: Banner of Truth Trust, 1969, first published in 1685)

Robertson, A.T.  _Word Pictures in the New Testament, General Epistles and Revelation_ (Nashville: Broadman Press: 1933)

Salmond, S.D.F.  "Jude"; _The Pulpit Commentary, Volume XXII_ (McLean, Virginia: MacDonald Publishing, ?)

Smith, David  "The Epistles of John" _The Expositor's Greek Testament, Volume V_ (London: Hodder and Stoughton Limited, ?)

Smith, Chuck  _New Testament Study Guide_ (Costa Mesa, California: The Word for Today, 1982)

Spurgeon, Charles Haddon  _The New Park Street Pulpit, Volumes 1-6_ and _The Metropolitan Tabernacle Pulpit, Volumes 7-63_ (Pasadena, Texas: Pilgrim Publications, 1990)

Stott, John R.W.  _The Letters of John_ (Grand Rapids: Eerdmans, 1988)

Townsend, Jim  _Epistles of John and Jude_ (Illinois: David C. Cook, Elgin, 1988)

Trapp, John  _A Commentary on the Old and New Testaments, Volume Five_ (Eureka, California: Tanski Publications, 1997)

Wiersbe, Warren W.  _The Bible Exposition Commentary, Volume 2_ (Wheaton, Illinois: Victor Books, 1989)

*With great pleasure, this book is dedicated to Nils-Erik and Gunnel Ingrid Bergström. Great thanks are due to the wonderful parents of my wife Inga-Lill, not only for raising a great daughter, but also for their graciousness and support over the years.*

*Once again I have happily depended on the proofreading help of Martina Patrick. It's just one more way that Martina and Tim show their kindness and friendship to us over many years. Thanks especially for all your prayers and support.*

*We use the same cover format and artwork for this commentary series, so continued thanks to Craig Brewer who created the cover and helped with the layout. Kara Valeri helped with graphic design. Gayle Erwin provided both inspiration and practical guidance. I am often amazed at the remarkable kindness of others, and thanks to all who give the gift of encouragement. With each year that passes, faithful friends and supporters become all the more precious. Through you all, God has been better to me than I have ever deserved.*

After more than 20 years of pastoral ministry in California, David Guzik and his family moved to Europe to became the director of Calvary Chapel Bible College Germany in July of 2003

David and his wife Inga-Lill live in Siegen, Germany with their children Aan-Sofie, Nathan, and Jonathan.

You can e-mail David at ewm@enduringword.com

For more resources by David Guzik, go to www.enduringword.com

# Also by David Guzik

## Verse-by-Verse Commentaries

Genesis (ISBN: 1-56599-049-8)
First Samuel (ISBN: 1-56599-040-4)
Second Samuel (ISBN: 1-56599-038-2)
Daniel (ISBN: 1-56599-036-6)
The Gospel of Mark (ISBN: 1-56599-035-8)
Acts (ISBN: 1-56599-047-1)
Romans (ISBN: 1-56599-041-2)
First Corinthians (ISBN: 1-56599-045-5)
Second Corinthians (ISBN: 1-56599-042-0)
Hebrews (ISBN: 1-56599-037-4)
1-2-3 John and Jude (ISBN: 1-56599-031-5)
Revelation (ISBN: 1-56599-043-9)

## Devotionals

Free and Clear (ISBN: 1-56599-033-1)
Near and True (ISBN: 1-56599-032-3)

## Software

New Testament & More (ISBN: 1-56599-048-X)
This CD-ROM gives immediate access to thousands of
pages of verse-by-verse Bible commentary through all of
the New Testament and many Old Testament books. For
ease of use, commentary is available in both Acrobat and
HTML format. Also includes bonus audio resources - hours
of David Guzik's teaching in mp3 format

# Find audio teaching by David Guzik at
# www.enduringword.com

CPSIA information can be obtained at www.ICGtesting.com
Printed in the USA
LVOW082230120312

272739LV00001B/67/A